Each Passing Moment

Each Passing Moment

The Path to Yourself: How to Find Peace, Meaning, and Fulfillment

Theodor Vik Andreas

Translated by George Chirita

Editor: Mihaela Sofonea

Cover design: Alexandru Neacsu

For my mother

Contents

1 | The Magical Hourglass

I stare at the small hourglass on my desk in awe. The sands of time are slowly but surely running low, and eventually, the top part of the hourglass will be completely empty.

I wonder how many tens of millions of seconds ran out from the hourglass of my life[1] in vain ambitions and illusions, chasing all sorts of goals that proved to be not that important and, sometimes, not even mine? Working myself to exhaustion while pursuing the next promotion or pay raise, trying to attain validation from those around me, tortured by the never-silent voice in my head ruminating on the events of the past, anticipating all the disasters that might happen to me, or just whispering that I'm not good enough. Living at a fast, hectic pace, unable to enjoy the small and simple pleasures of life. Checking off various activities on my daily to-do list, more or less important, while at the same time repeatedly procrastinating the self-reflection moments. A prisoner held captive in a life that sometimes seems unfamiliar to me, like it's someone else's, often trying to escape the cold reality by plunging into all sorts of silly, pointless, and numbing distractions. Surviving one more day just to start over again, having no idea about how I might build the life I dream of and a life that would be meaningful to me.

I wonder how many tens of millions of seconds went to waste, turning to ash, because I allowed myself to be self-centered, superficial, spiteful, lost in thoughts, sad, fearful, remorseful, or simply deciding that today, I'm not in the mood. Probably way too many.

I ask myself what it would be like if, at birth, each of us received a magical hourglass that measures the time we have on this Earth. What it would be like to see the sands of time running low, therefore being aware, each and every moment, that life is limited. That at a certain point in time, all will be over.

Would we treasure the present more, this instant in which we breathe, are alive, and can choose which way to go? Would it be easier to mute the infernal din of day-to-day life, discovering our own inner voice, realizing who we are and what we really want? Would we manage to build that life that grants us peace, meaning, and fulfillment? Or maybe, if we saw our time running low mercilessly, we would be engulfed by a feeling of emptiness, a terrible panic leaving us unable to act. Paralyzed.

I don't know what you think about this, but I, for one, would like such a magical hourglass. It would help me understand the importance of every second that passes by. The weight of every moment that cannot be recovered once gone.

2 | Emptiness

Living My Dream

From the outside, my life seemed perfect. Less than ten years after finishing college, I was reaping the fruits of my effort and perseverance: I was part of the middle-management team of a top company, earning an enviable salary and enjoying respect and appreciation in my field, with an even brighter future, considering the results—way above expectations—that I had delivered in the last two years. Debt-free and with a more than comfortable level of savings in my account. Involved for the past five years in a harmonious relationship with Simone, the one who would eventually become my wife. Get-togethers and lunches with the extended family, spending time with my dear nephew and godson, dinners and board game nights with our group of friends. And of course, the ever-present Facebook profile, with cool pictures taken on dream vacations to prove how well I was doing.

You would think that I was living the dream, but it did not seem to be my dream. I felt confused, uneasy, and lonely. I couldn't figure out why, and that only increased the level of my anxiety when the voice in my head was asking mockingly, "What's wrong with you?"

The Stairway to Success

It wasn't always like this. Up until I was almost thirty, the drive to prove my worth and succeed was an incredible fuel. I was always looking for new challenges, fighting until the last drop of energy and then pushing myself a little bit more, over that limit, achieving my goals and setting new and more ambitious ones. An infernal and all-consuming race to be better than everyone else. Until life became a game revolving around just a few words: *winning, more, never enough*.

I don't remember the exact moment when the first sign of discontent arose. It might have been on an ordinary Friday, when, at 9:00 p.m., going through the barrage of emails, I suddenly wondered, *What the hell am I doing with my life?* Or following a much-desired promotion and a well-earned bonus, when euphoria, pride, and self-importance quickly dissipated and left room for an inexplicable feeling of inner void. Surely I got rid of those thoughts immediately, blaming exhaustion.

Over time, there was a gradual accumulation of doubt, frustration, and dissatisfaction, and I tried my best to ignore these feelings. It's like when you make an effort to keep a semblance of neatness in your house, hiding the things one can see strewn around wherever you can. A box in the closet, some clothes in the wardrobe, a stack of magazines in the bookcase, and so forth, until there is not even an inch of unused space left, and you get to live in fear that, at any moment, the objects will overflow from their hiding places and crush you in an avalanche.

As I was climbing the corporate ladder, I felt that my inner world was collapsing. That I was sinking into a deep abyss. I often found myself overwhelmed by a feeling of emptiness. A fuzzy sensation that something was missing from my life. A vague sense that everything I had built was on shaky ground—a sandcastle by the sea. I was haunted by the possibility of a different kind of life, in which I could feel whole. But I did not know what I had to do to get there, and I was not willing to give up my ambitions and goals, nor anything that I had worked so hard to get.

Unhappiness

Looking at the people around me—relatives, friends, coworkers—I noticed similar unrest. Hidden by the bricks of their Facebook and LinkedIn walls that displayed an almost perfect life, behind the image of self-confidence that many of them were trying to project, I found many of the same symptoms that I was struggling with. The harrowing rush for everything life has to offer. The insatiable desire to capitalize on every opportunity to win or feel pleasure. The terrible dread of missing out. The ardent need to prove to those around them that they are better and stronger. A churning waterfall of moods, emotions, and impulses—hubris, envy, anger, greed, lust, stress, frustration, anxiety—they could not stand against, crushing any hope they ever had for happiness and peace.

The rest of the world didn't seem to do much better either. A while back, I used to like going to the city's central area at rush hour. I would find a place that was out of the way of the waves of the hundreds and thousands of people who were wandering around. I would listen to the hustle and bustle of the crowd, watching the faces of the ever-hurried passers-by: seriousness, irritability, restlessness, sadness, helplessness, submission. And very few smiles, way too few.

Were those considered elite luckier? Over time, I'd had the chance to meet men and women who, by society's standards, were seen as successful people and role models: they had money, fame, social standing. The cunning and self-satisfied smile, the words spoken with a hint of arrogance, and the condescending attitude were samples of the absolute success they were enjoying. Yet, the emptiness in their eyes seemed to tell a different story. The story of lives filled with luxury, exotic vacations, validation, and admiration, but depleted of inner peace, meaning, and fulfillment. The story of shiny shells on the outside that are hollow on the inside.

I sometimes felt overcome by a strange solace in thinking that I might not be the only unhappy person on Earth.

Live the Moment

For most of my adult life, I have chased success and happiness. Resolute, perseverant, never-yielding. Applying all that society and present-day culture teach us. Despite the achievements I've had and the progress I've made, I felt increasingly lost—a wanderer in the desert.

And suddenly, it hit me: I was simply burned out. How did I not realize it sooner? I pushed myself too hard. Trying to make more of everything. Working too much, too hard, with not enough breaks. Striving to win other people's approval. Forcing myself to always be in control. Being satisfied with nothing short of perfection. The ultra-productive employee, the flawless manager, the ideal partner, the model brother, the cool uncle, the best friend you could have. The conclusion could not be simpler. I had to apply the advice that I'd read dozens of times in magazines and books. Detach. Let loose. Enjoy life. Live the moment.

And that is what I did. I quit my well-paid job and started to live. Spontaneously, without a certain plan, without an agenda, embracing everything the moment brought. Zen. Nights of TV series and movies, days of lying on the beach and reading philosophy and detective novels, weekends in nature, going out for coffee with a friend at 11:00 a.m., savoring a romantic dinner with Simone in the middle of the week, paying a surprise visit to my parents, spending the afternoon with my nephew, or going out for a jog. Life was great. I felt relaxed, calm, at ease. Zen.

This did not last more than six months. It was fun to live with no purpose, no stress, no pressure, and no demands, dedicating my time to whatever I wanted to do instead of what I needed to do. Until it got boring. When you have in front of you a box with the best chocolates in the world, the first piece of chocolate lifts you in an incredible whirlwind of pleasure. The second piece of chocolate melts in your mouth with an explosion that numbs your senses. If you continue to eat, with each additional piece of chocolate, the pleasure fades, and by the time you get to the seventh piece, you're already queasy.

In a similar but inexplicable way at the time, the initial state of ease, peace, and joy—caused by embracing a hedonistic lifestyle—gradually evaporated. All my life, I've been dominated by a hidden feeling that I need to work hard, contribute, and conquer success. To provide undeniable proof of my worth to the whole world. Inactivity and lack of a sense of purpose had generated a state of dissatisfaction that simmered and imperceptibly turned into frustration and self-loathing.

I was once again fighting the feeling that something important was missing from my life.

Hitting the Snooze Button

The crisis I was facing was also augmented by the uncertainty of the steps I needed to take next. I had tried different paths and ended up in the same place every time. Unhappy, confused, aimless. Dropped into a bottomless pit. I felt that an essential piece of my life's puzzle was slipping through my fingers. I was looking for answers to questions that were floating mysteriously above my head, questions that I wasn't able to articulate. Both hopeful and fearful, I felt that I was at a crossroads that could mean my salvation if I should discover what I needed to do next. At the same time, I was consumed with envy when witnessing the professional and financial success that some of my peers enjoyed. Comparing my situation with theirs, the decision to quit my job now seemed a fatal error. A huge step backward. The temptation to rejoin the race and reclaim my position grew stronger every day.

With my eyes fixed on the grand prize—money, status, and success—I took a job at a top tech company, where I surpassed all my previous achievements in the years that followed.

Life had triggered an emergency alarm, and I decided to hit the snooze button. At the end of my hedonistic period, I thought I had reached rock bottom and that I could not sink any deeper. That the only way I could go was up. I didn't know at the moment that life had other plans.

3 | Nothingness

Desolation

Silence at the other end of the line. I thought he did not understand me, and I asked if he wanted me to repeat what I'd said. My friend, a medical doctor by trade, to whom I had just read my mother's computed tomography (CT) scan results, replied that there was no need for that. He continued with a hollow voice, seemingly a tad uncertain. It didn't sound very good. Because he hadn't seen the CT scan, he couldn't be 100 percent sure and recommended we go to the doctor as soon as possible.

After a few dreadful days, we had the confirmation: my mother's cancer had relapsed. After the surgery—the second in the last three years, the fourth overall—she had started chemotherapy and radiotherapy. Her optimism overflowed and reached us as well. We were hoping that things would fall into place, like all the other times. The treatment seemed to work, and gradually, life returned to relative normality. For me, that meant being stranded again between two parallel hells: one consisting of habits and instinctual reactions, chasing success and pleasure, and another in which I was plunging into an infinite void.

One year after the surgery, unforeseen and to everyone's amazement, including the doctors', the disease took an unexpected turn. Although much more aggressive, the treatment proved ineffective this time around. My mother's enfeebled body could not handle the poison injected into it any longer; thus, the doctors stopped the medication. Less than four months after the first signs of aggravation, following a period of unutterable suffering, my mother passed away.

...

The door is closed. I hear Dad's voice. He is calling our relatives to let them know. He bursts out crying every time he says, "Dora is dead."

∞

The funeral is the next day. In the evening, we leave the chapel, and I enter a small neighborhood shop with my sister. On our way to our parents' house, she tells me that she can't fully grasp that Mom is no longer with us, like she's not dead but gone to a faraway place. An illusory thought that gives us a temporary respite. We remember how, when we were kids, we were heading back home together, carrying the grocery bags that seemed huge to us, trying to guess what our mother had cooked for dinner.

Climbing the stairs, I feel a solid knot in my stomach. I can barely breathe at the thought that every time I used to come over, the door would open wide, and my mother would stand there eagerly waiting for us. Smiling.

∞

The coffin is slowly lowered into the grave, and the undertakers begin to cover it. The people gathered there start to leave one by one until I am left alone. The black and cold soil merges with the coffin with a muffled sound—like a sob.

∞

I feel exhausted, drained, numb. Lying on my bed, I hold one of my mother's sweaters close to my chest. A calm breeze engulfs me, and it's like I feel her caring presence close by. I am desperately clinging to this feeling without being able to grasp it. It seems that my mother's spirit is starting to fade away, further and further, until it disappears completely. All I want is to sleep, and maybe when I wake up, everything will turn out to be just a bad dream.

∞

Saturday, 4:40 p.m. Exactly one week ago, my mother drew her last breath. I am sitting in her bedroom, crushed by pain, reciting a prayer. My dad shows up and hugs me.

∞

My four-year-old nephew comes close to me. He seems solemn and pondering. He is holding some flowers. He shows them to me and tells me they are for his dead grandmother. I stick my fingernails deep into my flesh and force myself to stop the flood of tears.

...

A world in which the seas have dried. In which the sun no longer rises. Shattering desolation.

Reclusive

A few weeks had passed already. Every day, I would get up, take a shower, force myself to eat something, and go to work. I was avoiding small talk as best I could. People around me were a little uncomfortable, like they didn't know how to talk to me. Their sympathetic glances reminded me of what I wanted to forget. "How are you? Hang in there! You'll get through this ordeal." The effort of forcing a smile was agonizing, real torture.

I was afraid to open up, even in front of my closest friends. I didn't know how to be vulnerable, and I was striving to mask my frailty and pain by projecting a serene maturity of wise acceptance. But on the inside, I felt like a mirror shattered into hundreds of pieces. This discrepancy made me feel deceitful.

Conversations on any topic seemed meaningless, and the obligation to politely and gracefully contribute to the dialogue was drawing every last bit of energy out of me. To simplify, the interactions with people around me were causing me significant discomfort. For this reason, I chose to close myself within, to limit and avoid, as much as possible, any connection to and participation in social life.

Disconnected

I was ravaged by a devastating tornado that was wreaking havoc. Torn apart by the ordeal—still fresh in my mind—my mother had to endure during her last months of life. Enraged by the ruthless fate and the grave injustice that had befallen us. Blaming God for His cruelty and indifference. Continuously ruminating on the unfolding events and accusing myself, thinking that maybe I didn't do everything in my power to save her. Incapable of helping my father and my sister, each one trapped in his or her own nightmare. An overwhelming mix of feelings and sensations that I could not even identify or name at the time. Let alone manage them. The only bearable moments were the few hours of sleep during the night when I could afford the luxury of not being conscious of anything. Oblivion.

Today's culture teaches us all sorts of things about how to conquer the outside world and very little or next to nothing about taming the demons that haunt us in our darkest hours. Vulnerability is often mistaken for weakness. That is why the thought of asking for help terrifies us, and we prefer to handle problems on our own, as best we can. The advice, the methods, and the recipes we apply are often poorly suited to the difficulty of the turning point we are facing. What doesn't kill you makes you stronger. Fake it till you make it. Forge your way through the pain. Superficial bandages applied with negligence to a deep cut bleeding profusely.

I decided I needed to push forward, and the only option I saw was to ignore my feelings. To repress them. To disconnect from them.

Broken

I have always fought fiercely to be in control. Not to be taken by surprise by anything fate can throw at me. To anticipate and prevent what could go wrong. Like an algorithm that automatically compiles: if A, then B, else C. Life was starting to show me that I was deluding myself, but I was not yet prepared to give up the illusion that I could keep everything under control. So I took refuge in my work.

I was pushing harder than ever, taking on even more responsibilities and projects. Video conference with Asia at 8:00 a.m., the "scrum" meeting with my team, different emails and activities checked, sessions with my boss to present the ongoing projects, more emails and activities checked, negotiations, unexpected calls, averting a minor crisis, video conference with North America at 8:00 p.m., more emails and activities checked, a short call to Australia at 11:00 p.m. I was voluntarily pushing myself to the limit.

Eventually, I started to feel a dull pain in my left lung, which persisted for weeks. I decided to go to the doctor. The test results suggested that I was healthy. The pain continued to bother me, but I ignored it. A few months later, I developed symptoms of a cold that I treated with an infusion of vitamins, tea, and medication recommended by the pharmacist. When I started to dry-cough, I checked with a second doctor who, like the first one, found nothing wrong. After she asked me whether I had gone through a high-stress period, I summarized my recent past events. She patiently explained that distress and turmoil can sometimes cause physical reactions in the body.

I chose not to pay any more attention to these states, hoping they would subside. In a desperate attempt to distract myself, I sank even deeper into my work. In my everyday life, I was busy, active, always checking activities off my to-do list. I was surpassing all my previous achievements, and I was rapidly climbing the ladder of professional success. But inside, I was feeling defeated.

The layer of emptiness that had enveloped me for so many years and that I thought to be my rock bottom was broken. Subtly, I was sinking into an ocean of helplessness, hopelessness, and despair.

...

In our favorite movies or books, the main characters often face a critical moment, sending them lower than they thought they could go. Filled with doubt and hopelessness, despite the chances being stacked against them, they manage to bounce back, surprisingly emerging a victor in the final confrontation. This was not the image I had in my mind. I felt broken. Like an elastic band already stretched to its limit that you try to pull a few more inches.

...

When the rain starts pouring down from ominous black clouds, in cold torrents, when lightning splits the sky with its eerie light, and thunder breaks the silence with a deafening and frightening sound, nothing seems to indicate that the rain will soon stop and the sun will shyly emerge.

4 | Awakening

A Ray of Hope

It was a Sunday. The warm autumn sun radiated gently. More than one year had passed since my mother was no longer among us, but the wound was still open, fresh, unhealed. I approached the grave and placed the chrysanthemum bouquet near the cross. A few tears rolled down my cheek, and with them, the feeling of weight pressing on my shoulders—which I'd had each time on my way to the cemetery—lifted. The anticipation of a painful get-together.

I started, as always, by telling her what was new. What Simone, my dad, and my sister were up to. Sharing my little nephew's latest shenanigans. How he asked me, puzzled and intrigued, if he still needed to wash his hands if he managed to pee without touching his wee-wee. That, at work, everything was going according to plan. I asked her to stop worrying about us because we were fine. I felt the need to mention: we are trying to be fine. I didn't want to lie to her, but what good could have come if I told her that I was about to reach boiling point, ready to crack?

Suddenly, a troubling thought overwhelmed me: my mother would have been terribly sad to see me in the deplorable state I was in. A burning desire lit inside me. I needed to come to terms with what happened. To set myself free from the burden that was suffocating me. The burden of nothingness and emptiness. I hadn't even the faintest idea how I could do that or where to start. All I felt was that life had triggered another emergency alarm and that, this time, I was determined not to hit, out of habit, the snooze button.

Facing Death

We live in the grip of frights and anxieties. We fear many things. But most of all, we fear old age, disease, suffering, and death. We are terrified. When such thoughts cross our minds, we succumb to panic, like a mountain climber caught in a raging storm, unable to take another step. For most of us, the only way to cope with the disintegration that patiently awaits us at the end of the road is by avoiding such sinister ideas. How can we continue to create our future on the hope of the days to come when every passing day pushes us one step closer to the end? The most convenient answer is this: living like we doubt the existence of death.[2] We see its shadow all around us, and we prefer to take cover under the illusion that it will elude us for a long time to come.

When we deny life's impermanence and unpredictability, we only deny reality. Our loved ones will be taken away from us sooner or later, one by one, until death pulls our names out of the bag. Life is fragile, like a snowflake melting in the palm of your hand; fleeting, like a fire that burns brightly before slowly and silently dying out. We can try to fool ourselves that it is not so and live as if we were immortal, drifting on the tides of chance and destiny. Or we can look death straight in the eye and face it. Make peace with it. Accept it.

...

The first few times I did a visualization and contemplation exercise of my own disintegration,[3] I felt uncomfortable, flooded with fear and anxiety about the unknown. But I continued to practice it, and at one point, the fear was replaced by a subtle state of inner calm. Like the delicate flutter of a butterfly's wings. If you think this exercise is not for you, you can just skip it.

Here is the exercise: I find a quiet place where I can be alone and feel safe. I sit in a chair or lie on a bed, whichever is more comfortable. I close my eyes, and for a few minutes,

I focus my attention on my breath. I breathe in and slowly count to three. I hold the air in my chest for a second, and then I slowly breathe out, counting to three. I repeat this at least ten times. I feel my mind entering a state of respite.

I imagine walking in a graveyard. This is not a scary image for me; quite the opposite, the place seems serene. A tombstone catches my eye—my name is written on it. I recognize my birth year, but the year of my death is blurry. I run my fingers over my name and understand that all will be over someday. I allow this thought to sink in. I am not afraid—death is a natural part of life. I am facing my own mortality. I accept it. I touch the thin line separating the years that mark my beginning and my end. This small sign includes all of my existence. All my dreams and wishes, hopes and fears, achievements and disillusions, joys and sorrows, actions and indecisive moments, successes and failures. I'm pondering the evanescence of life. Nothing lasts forever; nothing is unending.

I bring my attention back to my breath for a few minutes. I open my eyes.

Managing Difficult Emotions

When hardship and suffering hit us, we are overwhelmed by a mixture of feelings: anger, guilt, unhappiness, grief. Instinct dictates that we have to run away from them. That the only way not to get knocked down and to survive is to reject them. To hide them in the nooks and crannies of our minds and pretend they don't exist. That they have never existed. We strive to go on and come back to the "normality" of days past. Like nothing happened. The solution proves to be inadequate and breeds a feeling of inauthenticity that estranges us from ourselves. The difficult emotions we try to bury in the pits of our soul emerge from the depths in unpredictable and uncontrollable ways. As if breaking up into pieces, they invade every cell of our bodies until we are pulled into a whirlwind of despair and helplessness.

Trials and tribulations are part of life. As much as we try to prevent bad things from happening, sometimes we find ourselves in situations we have limited control over. When we accept that the idea of total control is but an illusion, a new door opens, and through that door, we find the key to our healing. We understand that suffering is an inevitable component of the human condition. And that the only way to overcome an emotional shock, in a healthy way, is to face it. To open up to whatever we experience, even if it's painful. To embrace our own frailty and vulnerability, even if it's uncomfortable.[4]

...

For some, therapy works. They pour their soul out to the stranger in front of them—talking about difficult, long-passed events that still haunt them in their nightmares; uncovering deep wounds they didn't even know about; investigating the things they repeatedly said to themselves until they became convinced that they were true; discussing their feelings and emotions with a dose of curiosity.

Others, like me, turn to meditation and self-reflection. They learn to mute the uproar and chaos of day-to-day life and take refuge in the silence of their inner self—in the solitary silence of meeting oneself. They no longer reject the nothingness they drowned in for such a long time. They let it engulf them and immerse themselves in it. Acceptance brings forth clarity. They become capable of seeing the mixture of brutally repressed emotions. Guilt. Sadness. Anger. Helplessness. Desolation. Hopelessness. Patiently and mindfully, they turn their attention to each sensation, analyzing how it manifests within the body—without pushing it away or wishing to send it back to the vacuum it came from. Fast heartbeat. Palms and feet become cold as ice. A knot in the stomach. Tension in the neck and back muscles. Shaky breath. They observe each emotion appearing, growing in intensity, and then disappearing, like a wave breaking on the shore. "A passing state of mind."[5]

...

The void left by my mother's death was never filled. I catch myself looking at her picture on my desk. Sometimes with regret, wishing I could change the past. Other times, with a slightly nostalgic smile while remembering a pleasant moment or thinking how much joy she would have felt due to a recent event in our family. Maybe the pain will never completely disappear. And that's okay. I am no longer forcing the feeling to go away—pushing to be "normal."

I am grateful for all the moments we spent together, good and bad. I think that we were lucky, somewhat strangely. I was seven when the terrible affliction attacked my mother for the first time. Death had pulled her name out of the bag then but changed its mind, thinking maybe it wasn't her time yet.

What happens after we die? Does the soul keep on living? Maybe, I don't know. But she is always with me. In my memories. In my heart.

Closer to the Core

We live under the impression that we are at the center of the universe. That everything surrounding us—people, nature, and things—is nothing else but props in a mega-production in which we have the leading role. It's all about us—about our objectives, discontents, frustrations, dramas, achievements, and satisfaction. Nothing else matters. We take anything that happens personally. Even a simple rain seems an attempt to ruin our day. Sometimes we find ourselves thinking that the whole world is against us. The pressure we feel is very high, and we believe nobody can understand what it's like to be in our shoes.

During meditation, contemplating the concept of impermanence[6] and the transient nature of all that is, I was struck by a banal thought: nothing lasts forever. Human history is an unbroken chain of successive events. Kings, great conquerors, and heroes are born and die. Empires are built and end up being conquered or falling. Epochs change. Time flows impassively. The universe existed hundreds of millions of years before I was born and will continue to exist hundreds of millions of years after I'm gone. The years I have on this Earth are but a small dot on the axis of time. Nothing lasts forever. Without understanding how or why, this thought triggered moments of inner peace from which an unknown emotion was born. A strange mixture of unease and pure happiness. For the first time in my life, I felt that I was shedding the superficial layers of my existence and getting closer to the core.

Strangely, the terrible suffering I'd been through led me on a new path. Almost drowning in an ocean of despair and hopelessness, I somehow managed to reach the shore. I knew that I was no longer the person I used to be. I was prepared to take the next step. To plunge into the bottomless pit and face the emptiness that had held me captive countless times. To understand its origin.

The journey to myself had just begun.

5 | Awareness

Chasing Happiness

The result of my little experiment was revealing. I made a list of twenty people I know, making sure I included a diversified group with regard to age, sex, and professional and personal background, and asked them what their major objectives in life were. In other words, what they hoped to attain in the limited time they have on this Earth. Fourteen of them took me seriously. Everyone answered flatly that they wanted to be happy and fulfilled. When I asked what this meant for them, after an initial pause, they let loose an avalanche of clichés and goals for the following one, five, or ten years. A happy family, a successful career, a better-paying job, the respect and admiration of everyone around them, a sexy body, a second vacation house, a new sports car, different gadgets or things, exotic trips, starting their own business, taking a sabbatical, participating in a marathon or triathlon.

I realized that they, too, were prisoners in the same trap as I was. Wishing to conquer an inner state of peace and fulfillment by accumulating an endless stream of pleasant experiences and things. To gain this or that. To be one way or another. Convinced that as they procure more of anything and everything, they will inch closer to their dream destination: happiness.

How did we get here?

Primal Instincts

For thousands and thousands of years, our ancestors lived under the rule of urges and instincts. Allowing "fear, hunger, and sex"[7] to manipulate them, they managed to survive and reproduce.[8] The ever-vigilant individuals, anxiously thinking how to increase their food supply or how to strengthen their shelter, had a better chance of surviving than the less prudent individuals who preferred to take it easy, thus risking dying due to hunger or being eaten by a wild animal. The individuals who managed to gather resources enjoyed a privileged status within the tribe, therefore being able to strengthen their relationships with the other members, to gain their support and increase their own influence and power. The individuals who made efforts to consolidate their social status had a better chance of staying alive and successfully mating than the individuals who were not interested in winning the popularity contest. The latter risked becoming the group's weak link and could be easily bereft of their possessions, banished from the tribe, or even killed.

The never-ending chase for "more," the need to get validation and social status, the impulse to satisfy their insatiable and selfish desires—all these proved to be essential for our ancestors' survival. These primal instincts are deeply rooted in us, configured in the modern human's brain, leaving a mark on the values and motivations on which we choose to build our existence.

Living on Autopilot

According to a recent survey conducted by the University of California, 73.2 percent of first-year students declared that they were going to college to make more money. When asked what their main personal objectives were, 84.3 percent said they wanted to "be very well off financially," and just 49.8 percent considered that "developing a meaningful philosophy of life" was a worthy purpose.[9] Another survey showed that half of the young adults surveyed, aged eighteen to twenty-five, valued fame.[10]

Beginning in childhood, we are enrolled in the race for success.[11] From the first years of school, we learn that the role of education is not to help us discover new and mysterious horizons but to allow us to build the foundation for a prosperous future. Do we want to have a high-paying job when we grow up? Then we need to study hard and get good grades. A B+ is sufficient as long as no one else got an A. And an A is not quite as valuable if five other classmates got it. We notice that hardworking students enjoy a privileged status in the teacher's eyes, and many times, our parents say we should follow their example. Driven by the terrible fear of disappointing them and the burning desire to receive praise, we keep studying as best we can. We hang on, thinking of our next weekend. A good result on a difficult test brings us joy and tremendous relief, which are swiftly replaced by the anxiety of preparing for the next exam. Generally, we are proud of our achievements. Full of conceit, we regard the students who get poor results with a mixture of pity, arrogance, and contempt. When we receive a low grade, we have an acute end-of-the-world feeling. The Apocalypse. Overwhelmed with shame, terrified by what other people might think, with envy toward those who outperformed us this time, angry with ourselves for the deplorable performance, we start doubting our qualities.

By the time we finish high school, our set of values and motivations is well formed. We are defined by our skills and talents, by the successes, status, and popularity that we achieve. The self-image we project around us and other people's opinions of us matter. Appreciation validates us, whereas critiques—or, worse, indifference—are a clear indication that we are not good enough. The pie is limited, and if we want to get a bigger slice, we have to compete aggressively. Winning entails continuous effort. Success is possible only if we are willing to sacrifice the present and work hard to increase our chances of getting where we want to be. To fail in one particular endeavor is synonymous with being a loser. Happiness and self-fulfillment are conditioned by obtaining as many external victories as possible.

In college and then in our jobs, we continue to apply and perfect the recipe for success. We always have an eye on the next promotion or pay raise. As we advance, the competition becomes fiercer. We spend more and more energy improving our professional skills. We squeeze the benefits from every opportunity that arises until they're dry. We desperately promote our achievements, trying to impress as many people as possible. A wave of pride and superiority floods us when we introduce ourselves, mentioning the company we work for and the position we hold there.

The Dead End

We continue to work hard. Each time we attain a goal, we allow ourselves to relax and enjoy the moment. But the satisfaction proves to be short-lived. We quickly get used to the new situation that, not long ago, seemed to be the Nirvana we yearned for. Without lingering too much on it, we set a new target, even more ambitious.

Years go by, and we feel more and more trapped in this race against the clock. Always busy; always assaulted by all sorts of requests, demands, and favors; always checking off one more activity that needs to be done at the office or at home. Besides the moments when something extraordinary happens, we live submerged in a sea of boredom. We say to ourselves that all we need is a long weekend or a vacation with our family, which passes in no time, leaving us with the same dull feeling of insufficiency. As if our lives are incomplete. We look back on the road we've traveled, interspersed with many victories, and we realize that we forgot our destination. Like an amnesiac who, at the end of the day, does not remember why he did what he did but is prepared nonetheless to start over the next day.

Sometimes we are enveloped by a vague doubt that— driven by improper motivations—we chased superficial values. That because we were so preoccupied with projecting the perfect life on the outside, we did not manage to discern what is essential. The buzzing of our phone dispels the dream. We breathe in, take a sip of coffee, and force ourselves to get rid of these dark and unpleasant thoughts. We have lots of work to do.

The Hedonistic Cocktail

The harder we try to ignore our inner turmoil and pretend that everything is all right, the deeper we sink into an existential crisis that we are not equipped to recognize and manage. After all, in college and throughout our careers, we become experts in areas like finance, medicine, marketing, IT, and so forth. We can talk for hours on end about our jobs and our fields. In contrast, we are incoherent and confused about our inner lives. It's no wonder that we mistake the existential crisis for an advanced state of numbness most of the time.

We sense the need to detach. To forget about the world and feel that the world has forgotten about us. To mute its deafening noise. Not to think about our career, ambitions and projects, family, finance and loans, problems, and other people's expectations of us. Not to be required to analyze, assess, and make decisions. No cares, stresses, and anxiety. No plans and long-term goals. We feel a pressing desire to feast on life's nectar and experience its pleasures. We convince ourselves that this is the medicine we need to end this state of inertia.

The hedonistic cocktail[12] is unique for each of us. Some, like me, quit their jobs and live with no plan. Others try desperately to remove the word *must* from their vocabulary, reaching a point where they completely ignore their professional and family responsibilities. Quite a few resort to eccentric or exaggerated acquisitions: they buy a vacation house or a sports car they cannot afford; they renew their wardrobe, adding extravagant and expensive apparel. Alcohol, free and uninhibited love, extramarital relationships, drugs, and gambling are the ingredients that others feel they need to shake them out of this state of numbness.

In limited doses and for short periods, without hurting ourselves or those around us, without endangering our long-term objectives, health, relationships, career, and financial stability, a moderately hedonistic behavior that excludes any harmful activity—for example, extramarital sexual activities, drugs, and gambling—can briefly recharge our batteries.[13] A temporary alleviation, perhaps, but one that doesn't offer a real solution for overcoming the existential crisis.

People who lack self-control risk ending up as slaves to the pleasures they indulge in. Urges are endless and lead to addiction. Every time we satisfy a desire, the moment of ecstasy passes, and the urge reappears, stronger and more insatiable. Lacking moderation, we slip on a dangerous slope, where the fall can accelerate, generating consistent and sometimes irreversible damage.

At the end of the hedonistic experience, we don't find the happiness we dreamed we would. Just a bottomless pit. Emptiness.

Quiet Desperation

Recent studies seem to show that Thoreau was right when he said that "the mass of men lead lives of quiet desperation."

...

Between 2007 and 2017, the number of people suffering from depression increased globally by 14 percent, up to a total of 264 million. The number of people afflicted by anxiety disorders increased by 12 percent, up to a total of 284 million.[14]

The depression rates show an increasing trend in the United States as well. Even more disturbing is the fact that many young people between the ages of twelve and seventeen face this affliction: 13 percent of the adolescents surveyed experienced at least one major depressive episode in 2017, compared with 8 percent in 2007.[15]

The general well-being of Americans has deteriorated constantly over the last twenty years: thirteen out of one hundred people said they were unhappy in 2018, compared with just eight out of a hundred in 1990.[16] Considering that wealth—represented by the gross domestic product per capita—increased by 164 percent in the same period,[17] we need to ask ourselves, What's going on?

…

These numbers are quite alarming. We live in one of the most prosperous times in history. As a society, we enjoy both comfort and a standard of living that just twenty years ago would have seemed like science fiction. We can retrieve any information we need in a few seconds; for every necessity, we can easily find dozens of products and services to choose from; we can communicate anytime, with anyone, no matter where they are; we have continued access to water and electricity, air-conditioned houses, and all sorts of smart gadgets; if we want, we can travel around the world in three or four days, and it won't cost us a fortune. The examples could go on and on.

Yet despite the unimaginable progress, it looks like we became unhappier.

The Illusion of Happiness

The formula on which we are taught to build our happiness

is flawed. Up to a point, it's normal to look for money and social validation or to dream of pleasant experiences. These are necessary, in a certain dose, for a happy life. But beyond a specific level that guarantees our family's safety, security, and comfort, these components are not enough. Multiple studies show this.

Psychologist Daniel Kahneman and economist Angus Deaton concluded that for an American who makes more than $75,000 per year, there is no improvement in emotional well-being to be attained with a higher salary, which means an annual income of more than $75,000 will not make him or her happier.[18]

Another study showed that despite the initial euphoria, lottery winners returned to their initial state of happiness a few months after they won.[19]

We are all victims of the phenomenon psychologists call "hedonic adaptation." We want, and we get what we want. To our surprise, the joy quickly fades. We end up miserable and unhappy, wishing for something else—more of it, better, more pleasant, more satisfying. Held captive in this infinite spiral that helped our ancestors survive but that proves to be ineffective for us, modern people, in our attempt to attain happiness.

...

Jim Carrey said it best: "I think everybody should get rich and famous and do everything they ever dreamed of so they can see that it's not the answer."

6 | The "Aha!" Moment

The "Aha!" moment can come on an ordinary day, while we are flipping through a book or watching a movie. A stroke of wisdom. Or months, even years, after a tragic event, when we understand the lesson that destiny was trying to teach us. It's not about a moment of sudden enlightenment in which we gain supreme knowledge and access to the absolute truth. It's about realizing that we lived on autopilot, mindlessly setting and appropriating all sorts of goals that we doggedly chased. That we explored too little—or maybe not at all—a few of the major questions. Perhaps the most important ones.[20] What matters to me? What is the meaning of my existence? What do I need to do to enrich my inner world? How can I attain peace of mind and fulfillment?

We cannot hope to find default solutions. Because there are no absolute, complete, and irrevocable answers. All we can do is embark on a quest for knowledge and wisdom with an unknown destination. Understanding that no matter what conclusions we reach, not taking the time to investigate and meditate on these fundamental questions is to condemn ourselves to live a shallow and superficial life. Insufficient. Unfulfilled.

7 | Mastering Desire

Up to a certain point in life, I had been dominated by my desires, letting them take me wherever they pleased. Trying, always unsuccessfully, to fill the void that I felt inside by buying and accumulating, surrendering to impulses, and satisfying my urges.

Recognizing this, I said to myself that it was a perfect starting point: understanding how I could tame my desires. A first step—small but important.

I Compare Myself; Therefore I Am

The person driving a Honda wants to buy a BMW, like his neighbor across the street. That neighbor envies her boss, who owns a Ferrari. The boss dreams about the day he can afford a helicopter, like his old college mate. That guy is motivated by the wish to have a private jet, like one of the majority shareholders in his company. And to top it all off, the majority shareholder wants, at least for a day, to put an end to all the meetings and deadlines and go to a park with her kids to ride a bike, as she promised them more than five months ago.

We pick up the habit of comparing ourselves to those around us from a young age. When we get a new toy car or a new doll, we are over the moon. But the second we see another child's toy, we become frustrated and unhappy. What we have no longer satisfies us, and we want a toy identical to that of the child we envy. As we grow up, we continue to relate to our friends and colleagues to draw conclusions about our own selves. As adults, the comparison with others is a well-anchored habit that we use to assess our achievements, success, and happiness.

...

Which of the two circles marked with 1 and 2 is larger?[21]

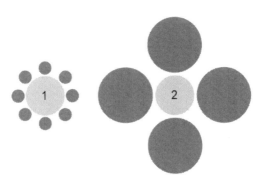

A lot of people choose circle number one. That answer is wrong. The two circles are identical. The size of the outside circles surrounding them—to which we measure the inner circles—changes the way we perceive reality.

...

All my life, I've been comparing myself to others. And quite a few times, I felt like the second circle. Small and insignificant. Torn by envy. Wishing for more, so I could feel like the first circle—big and important.

Some people see this constant comparison to those around them as motivation. I'll admit, that was the case for me too. It pushed me to act. But with a completely inadequate attitude. Tooth and nail, bitter, teeth grinding and fists clenched. All or nothing. Distraught with all that I didn't have yet, incapable of enjoying what I did have.

Maybe it would be better for our well-being to identify the persons we look up to, the decent folks living balanced and fulfilled lives, in order to find a source of inspiration in their success. And measure only against ourselves. If today we are just slightly better than we were yesterday, then the day was not wasted.

Gratitude

At my low point, I couldn't remember the last time I contemplated what was good in my life. What I earned through effort or what was simply given to me without requiring any contribution. The love, abundance, and opportunities I received. The small and simple joys of life.

It's not an exercise we often do. Some never do it. Usually, we take things for granted. The fact that we were born and raised in a country with no major conflicts. That we are healthy. That there is a comfy place we can call home. That we were nurtured by our parents or grandparents, who offered us a good education. That we live in a time of history when we have countless opportunities. That we are surrounded by people who care about us and love us. That we have a job, or maybe a business, that provides us with a decent standard of living. That we can afford to travel or follow our passions and hobbies. That we can go to the park on a beautiful spring day and admire the green nature, watch the blue sky, and feel the scent of blossoming trees; or that on a cold winter evening, we can sit clad in a blanket, savoring a cup of mulled wine and a delicious dessert. We are used to all this and think we simply deserve it. That we are entitled to it.

...

In 2017, 689 million people were living on less than $1.90 per day. Almost one in four people in the world needed to manage with less than $3.20 per day, and 43 percent of the world's population lived on less than $5.50

per day.[22]

Germany Kent, an American writer and journalist, said: "Take time daily to reflect on how much you have. It may not be all that you want but remember someone somewhere is dreaming to have what you have."

...

I took for granted too many moments spent with my mother. An extended family vacation, Christmas days, or lunch with loved ones on a random Sunday. Slightly bored or with my mind wandering, I did not completely savor the event, as if, subconsciously, I anticipated that there would always be a next time. I learned the hard way that we sometimes experience something for the last time without realizing it at the moment. That life can tear us apart, in the blink of an eye, from people, places, or things that we supposed we would have around for much longer. When I understood the principle of impermanence, when this evident truth was absorbed by every fiber of my being, I realized I could no longer afford the luxury of being ungrateful. That is why I decided to create a new habit: taking the time to reflect on the abundance and blessings in my life.

I would ask those who are frustrated that they don't yet have a six-figure income: What amount would it take to sell your sight, hands, or feet? What price would you put on the health of a loved one?

...

Some see gratitude as an obstacle to achieving success—a roadblock to progress. Because it could generate a state of complacency, self-contentment, or even resigned acceptance. But research suggests otherwise. According to psychologist Robert A. Emmons, who studied this topic, being grateful has numerous benefits, among which: it "increases self-esteem, enhances willpower, strengthens relationships, deepens spirituality, boosts creativity, and improves athletic and academic performance."[23]

Gratitude doesn't mean fooling ourselves that everything is all right and giving up our dreams but finding joy in how we live or what we have at the moment while continuing to aim for our next achievement. Like a mountain climber who stops here and there to admire the view from the newly conquered position without losing sight of the peak.

...

I was making slight progress in my attempt to untangle the mysteries of a meaningful life. The time had come to focus on a central theme that I had long neglected.

I couldn't get poor Christian—an acquaintance of Simone's—out of my mind. His drama resurfaced from the locked chest in which I had tried to stuff it years back.

8 | Purpose

The Absurdity of Existence

A few days before he killed himself, Christian had visited his parents' country house, the one he had grown up in. His mother and sister subsequently said that he had acted differently. He had been silent and lost in thoughts. He went for a few walks on the hills nearby, which he rarely did. Seeing their unrest, he tried to put them at ease by telling them he was all right and just a little tired. But his sad smile and melancholic eyes were betraying him. In the morning of the day he left for home, he woke up early and went to the cemetery where his father was buried. Upon his return, he didn't want any breakfast; he poured himself a cup of coffee and went outside, into the garden that opened toward the wooded hills. He smoked a cigarette. For twenty minutes, he just stood there, without making a move, and admired the view. He had probably already made his decision. He only came to say goodbye to his parents and the place where he grew up.

This image haunted me for days. A desolate view, with Christian seen from the back through the window frame. A frightened mother who feels her son's distress. The scattering cigarette smoke. A forty-year-old man—son, husband, and father—burdened by deep grief that only he knew of. A sad smile hiding a silent scream of desperation.

I had talked to him briefly over the phone a while back. I tried to remember that conversation dozens of times, attempting to recall every word, each voice modulation, and each pause, looking for a clue, however small. He spoke in a manner that sent optimistic vibes. He played his part well—an actor, with a smiling mask, who fails to find any more meaning in the play he was cast in, wishing to end it sooner.

A tragic end triggering a shock wave for all who knew him. On the outside, he seemed a joyful person. Making jokes and plotting pranks. A drama that gave birth to an endless stream of pain for his family members. A mother torn apart. An abandoned wife. A fatherless child.

...

Christian is not an isolated case. Every forty seconds, someone takes his or her own life.[24] In 2016, suicide was the second-leading cause of death for young people aged fifteen through twenty-nine, after car accidents.[25] Contrary to what we may think, rich countries have high rates of suicide.[26]

Humans are the only animal capable of suppressing their survival instinct and killing themselves.

...

Way too many of our fellow beings, facing the absurdity of existence in a universe that seems cold, random, and irrational, choose a dramatic and irreversible action.

Living every day and every moment with an inner suffering that many of us cannot conceive, they do not find a way to make their lives bearable. They cannot find a reason to be. For them, death appears as the only solution to escape the torment. To break loose from their existence.

Faith

Some people find relief and hope in their faith. They believe God created the universe, plants, and animals, including humans. God is infinite love, and all that happens in the world, good or bad, happens by His will for the salvation of our souls. Nothing is by chance. God has a plan for everything and everyone. The highest mountain and the smallest ant were designed for a purpose. Similarly, each of us was born by His will to live for the love of God, for the love of humanity, and His entire creation. The years we have on this Earth are a "temporary assignment," and death is not the final destination but a milestone for the soul's return to its true home—Heaven.[27]

For believers, the suffering, the injustice, and the evil in the world are all part of God's universal project that the limited mind of the human does not have access to—and even if it did, it couldn't comprehend it. The pieces of life that sometimes seem to defy our understanding are small elements that match perfectly in the divine construction. If we could see the entire masterpiece, we would discover the meaning of everything that's happening—the flawless logic of the world. But because of our status as inferior creatures forged by the supreme being, full knowledge and absolute truth are forbidden.[28]

Pure and lasting faith is a fire that burns brighter in the soul of the believer, melting the ice of the absurdity of existence. Faced with the inevitable trials and tribulations of life, believers are fortified by their love for God and their trust in God's boundless love for them. In the darkest and most challenging moments, they feel the divine presence and protection. They humbly accept their status without judging, without asking the whys and the hows. They understand that "the Lord gave and the Lord has taken away."[29] They abandon their lives in the hands of the Lord, being confident that good and love will triumph in the end.

...

Recent studies show that religious people tend to be happier.[30]

...

What about the people whose faith is not that strong, the ones grappling with questions and doubts, the ones who feel they are on their own in this cold and meaningless universe? How can they confront the absurdity of existence?

The Struggle

The French writer and philosopher Albert Camus is just one of the thinkers who reject the option of suicide. In the end, it only deepens the absurdity. How can one hope to cancel life's lack of meaning by a gesture that is in itself illogical and irrational?

For Camus, spiritual and religious life do not represent an alternative either. Some people wished and tried to understand, make a connection, initiate a dialogue with what is beyond human and the potential source of life. Maybe they didn't try hard enough; maybe they didn't search in the right place or at the right time; maybe they weren't yet prepared to receive the message. But it's clear that at the other end, they came across a wall of silence. It was hard for them to take a leap of faith. They certainly could have kept and practiced, at least mechanically, some rituals, but if they had done that, they would have felt that they were fooling the one they unsuccessfully looked for. Nevertheless, some days, they stop whatever they're doing, look up to the sky, and send out a good thought and a prayer for a loved one. They get no answer, and that's fine by them.

For Camus, rejecting both suicide and spiritual life, only one solution is left when facing the absurd. To accept it. To embrace it. To continue living, day after day, "unreconciled," without the comfort of a world beyond this one, without the solace of a possible Heaven. A lucid and defying act of protest against the nonsense of an existence that ends in disintegration and death.[31]

But how? How can we live without identifying with Sisyphus—pushing a boulder to the top of a mountain, just to see it toppling back down, forcing us to do the grueling work over and over again?

Man's Search for Meaning

The world's great minds have always wanted to find an answer to the question: What drives human beings? The theories are abundant. Is the individual motivated by pleasure and the primitive impulse to search for the instant satisfaction of any need and desire?[32] Or maybe the key factor is the ambition to overcome the feeling of inferiority that gives birth to the endeavor toward superiority. Present in each individual, this state pushes some to contribute to the common good and others to strive for power and domination.[33]

According to Viktor Frankl, the famous Austrian psychiatrist and psychotherapist, the supreme motivation is the need to find meaning. In other words, pleasure or power can be a fuel that sustains human activity, but beyond a certain point, they prove to be insufficient. To cross the existential abyss, one needs a purpose in life.

...

Frankl, Jewish by birth, survived the Nazi concentration camps, where he lost his wife, mother, father, and brother. A few things helped him endure what proved to be hell on Earth. One of them was the determination to rewrite the manuscript containing the fundamental concepts of the theory he had created, which the Nazis confiscated. Another was his wish to help the other inmates face the concentration camp's nightmare and, in the unlikely event he would survive, to share his experience with the rest of the world.

In his book *Man's Search for Meaning*, where he tells the story of his time in the concentration camp and the lessons he learned, Frankl asks: What can you offer a man who no longer sees a purpose in what he's living, who has lost the will to go on and says that life has nothing more to offer him? "What was really needed," Frankl writes, "was a fundamental change in our attitude toward life. We had to learn ourselves and, furthermore, we had to teach the despairing men, that it did not really matter what we expected from life, but rather what life expected from us. We needed to stop asking about the meaning of life, and instead to think of ourselves as those who were being questioned by life—daily and hourly. Our answer must consist, not in talk and meditation, but in right action and in right conduct. Life ultimately means taking the responsibility to find the right answer to its problems and to fulfill the tasks which it constantly sets for each individual."[34]

After his release from the concentration camp, Viktor Frankl continued with the mission and work that saved his soul. To help those around him find their unique meaning in their own existential circumstances.[35] To remind them that they can lose everything, except the freedom to decide how they act, and that, in the end, if they cannot change their surroundings, they have the option of changing their attitude toward what's happening to them.[36]

...

I don't think I ever seriously pondered how I could build an existence that meant something to me. I treated everything like a game: the only thing that mattered was to reach my target and unlock the next level. For other people, the world is another kind of game, in which the most important thing is to chase pleasure and have fun. There are quite a few people who believe that happiness means finding a balance between the two: "Work hard; party harder!"

...

From a certain age, if we pay attention, we subtly begin to feel the shadow of death that watches how the seconds run out from the hourglass of our lives, waiting to send its black angels to claim our souls when our time has come. However, death is not what we should be afraid of. Because our greatest enemy is the lack of "why." Living without knowing why.

Without a sense of purpose, we are like runners who haven't got the faintest idea where they want to go, racing around aimlessly. Leaves randomly scattered by the wind. Boats floating adrift. Without a sense of purpose, we will end up enveloped, sooner or later, by deep hopelessness when thinking that we didn't know how to live. That we didn't know what to do with the time we had—that we squandered it.

Confronted with the absurdity of existence, with the suffering whose purpose we cannot grasp, with old age, disintegration, and death, we are forced to look at the emptiness of life and understand that it will not have any meaning unless we give it one; that we need to take responsibility in capitalizing on the time we've been offered.

What Does Life Expect of You?

Most of our actions are fueled by the underlying logic, "What's in it for me?" This is a one-way road that leads to a dead end: selfishness. The unhappiest people are those who, obsessed with their satisfaction and happiness, think only of themselves. Incapable of understanding that fulfillment cannot be achieved if it's chased as a goal in itself.[37]

Fulfillment becomes possible only if we escape the limited thinking of the "me above all else" perspective and completely surrender to a project or mission larger than ourselves. Something important that really matters to us. Something we believe in with all our being. Writing a book, producing an independent movie, or setting up a painting exhibition to bring to life a world that only exists in our minds and that we want to share with others. Making a weekly show on social media to bring a touch of joy and a good mood to those around us. Launching a business that helps mom-and-pop stores promote themselves more effectively and survive the battle against corporations. Practicing as a lawyer to put our skills in the service of truth and good. Getting involved in the social or political life of our community because we are not satisfied with how things are going, and we believe that honest citizens must take action. Volunteering in humanitarian activities because of the desire to bring a little relief to the forgotten and the forsaken. Dedicating ourselves to a person we love or starting a family. Regardless of what we choose, we manage to silence the background noise, ignore society's expectations and the pressure of those around us, and courageously follow our principles, beliefs, and passions. We do not act as a result of being motivated by what might await us in the end—fulfillment, applause, admiration, fame, success, or money—but simply because the journey itself gives us meaning and joy.

There is no standard recipe or universally valid formula. Everyone must identify the solution that suits them in their existential context. Everyone must look for an answer to Viktor Frankl's question: What does life expect from you?

If Today Were the Last Day of Your Life

Our interests, passions, and values evolve with us. The things that mattered when we were twenty-five may seem trivial to us at thirty-five when we identify a new sense of purpose that we should use as a guide in the journey through life. Five, eight, or ten years later, we realize that we need to update our internal compass once more. And so on. There is nothing wrong with that. Change is the only constant. We just have to be mindful and become aware of when we need to reassess our priorities. To evaluate them. To prioritize them.

···

Steve Jobs: "For the past 33 years, I have looked in the mirror every morning and asked myself: 'If today were the last day of my life, would I want to do what I am about to do today?' And whenever the answer has been 'No' for too many days in a row, I know I need to change something."

···

We may find, at certain stages, that our situation does not allow us to make the radical changes necessary to realign ourselves to the new major goals that will bring us fulfillment. A forty-eight-year-old programmer, bored of writing lines of code that produce robots to replace people's jobs, may not have the choice to give up her job or career if she needs money to support her three children. But she can devote at least a few hours a week to activities in which she finds pleasure and meaning.[38] She can volunteer for a nongovernmental organization (NGO) that helps children with cancer and needs the services of a programmer. She can join a nonprofit association that offers free classes to the unemployed who want to retrain and provide services as an instructor. And at the same time, she can start working on the book she wanted to write ten years ago. The involvement in these projects, which are essential to her, will generate an infusion of joy and fulfillment.

...

I was debating with one of my friends the newly discovered ideas that had filled me with energy and optimism. He dryly replied that everything sounds beautiful, but it's just a great illusion at the end of the day. Because nothing we achieve matters in the grand universal scheme since our death voids whatever we do or do not do.

I replied with an argument that belongs to Viktor Frankl. Nothing is annulled in the past and history. The passage of time does not erase but preserves. No one and nothing can eliminate the lived experiences, even the negative ones, that you faced with "courage and dignity." The good and evil you have done can never be undone.[39]

So how will you choose to live your life?

9 | Living with Integrity

First Betrayal

I was four or five years old. I was playing in my kindergarten yard with Phillip, one of my friends. Without realizing it, we were surrounded by a group of about ten children. They started shouting at us and throwing the pebbles they had collected in their pockets. We tried to get out of their midst, but they wouldn't let us. They shoved us into the center of the circle, which had become even tighter, like a noose. Frightened, we dropped down to the ground and started crying. When they began shouting, "Whi-ny ba-bies! Whi-ny ba-bies," Phillip grabbed my hand, squeezing it hard. One of the popular girls, Olga, looked at me and told me that I hadn't done anything to her, that she wasn't upset with me, and that I could join them. Without losing a moment's thought, I got up and walked over to her. I wiped away my tears and joined the chorus of voices shouting at Phillip, "Whi-ny ba-by! Whi-ny ba-by!"

An event lost in the mists of time, which suddenly reappeared in my mind. As if it happened yesterday. When I remembered my gesture, I was overwhelmed by a wave of guilt and shame.

When I replay that scene in my head, I feel the squeeze of Phillip's hand. The boy who clung desperately to me, whom I abandoned. Crouching, crying, hiding his head between his knees. Amid the crowd of angry children whose gaze—a bizarre mixture of cruelty and joy—still pierces me.

The Predatory Instinct

Preserved within us is the primary hunting instinct inherited from our ancestors, an instinct that pushed us to the top of the food chain, at the end of a difficult road made over hundreds of thousands of years—a road littered with multiple collateral victims. The indisputable proof of human supremacy is the continuous, mindless, and unparalleled decimation of our own habitat. Since we started logging, 46 percent of the trees have been cut down.[40] One million species of animals and plants are on the verge of extinction due to humans.[41] The population of mammals, fish, birds, reptiles, and amphibians decreased by approximately 68 percent between 1970 and 2016.[42]

The unbridled desire for expansion, accumulation, and

power has fueled not only hostility against other species but also human hatred of fellow humans. Our history is marked by a long series of conflicts between individuals, tribes, and nations. Some estimates show that in the last 5,500 years, there have been more than 14,500 wars that have resulted in over 1.2 billion casualties.[43] In the twentieth century alone, about 231 million people died due to wars and conflicts.[44]

...

Albert Einstein: "The real problem is in the hearts and minds of men. It is not a problem of physics but of ethics. It is easier to denature plutonium than to denature the evil spirit of man."

...

We currently live in one of the most prosperous and peaceful times in history. Most countries around the world have democratic regimes built around fundamental values such as justice, truth, and the importance of every human being. In these regimes, the individual's rights and liberties are guaranteed and protected. Atrocities such as flogging, flaying, cutting limbs, or death by beheading—which just a few hundred years ago were accepted practices and sometimes were even punishments applied by state institutions—would shock us today and create waves of indignation and virulent civic reactions.

Yes, we have evolved a great deal. And yet, despite all this progress, in each one of us, there is still a latent remnant of our predatory instinct, which can surface at any time. It is true that most people, the overwhelming majority, actually, are not capable of murder, rape, robberies, and other such crimes. Nevertheless, we are frequently surprised to see that we act unexpectedly and unpredictably, instinctively guided by strong and hard-to-control temptations to accumulate, dominate, and satisfy our desires.

Dog Eat Dog

Competitiveness was one of the most important driving forces underlying the development of society. A catalyst for human action. The spirit of competition unleashed an unimaginable flow of energy that pushed us to aim high, trying to reach for the stars. In the last decades, however, things have gotten out of hand. The uncontrollable force that helped us triumph against all odds enslaved us and triggered a crisis of excesses. The competition today is fiercer than ever. Victory at any cost is our guiding principle. Second place, fair play, and the joy of being part of the race are considered elements of failure. An upside-down world that skews the perspective of the values we measure against.

Today, everything is judged simplistically from a pragmatic and economic point of view. The individual's contribution is measured exclusively by quantity—the number of hours worked and the level of productivity achieved. "To have" has become synonymous with "to be." Human identity is reduced to a series of superficial factors, such as the car we drive, the job title, the brands we wear or choose to decorate our homes with, the restaurants we frequent, or the cool pictures from our exotic vacations that we post on social media. We lose sight of the invisible and immeasurable elements that give us our true value: the beliefs we are guided by, the causes we fight for, and the principles we preserve in the most challenging moments.

Life turns into a simple zero-sum game in which everything around us—people and objects—is a mere resource that we can use to maximize our satisfaction and gains. This environment is perfect for the predator within us to surface and make sure we get our hands on as big of a slice of pie as possible. We apply double standards, holding other people accountable to a set of demanding criteria we ourselves often fail to meet. We rationalize this by using beautiful and carefully chosen words, and at the same time, we easily dismiss others' apologies. In order to achieve our goals, we relinquish the guiding principles and things we believe in, and we constantly adjust our points of view and actions, depending on what best fits the circumstances in which we find ourselves. We consider that we are agile and flexible, but in reality, we turn into cunning individuals, devoid of all internal consistency, who often agree to compromise, thus ending up compromised. We try to take as much and offer as little as possible, and in extreme situations, or when the stakes are high, we are willing to behave ruthlessly and step on others. We congratulate ourselves for the fact that we take advantage of every opportunity, that we are persuasive and skilled negotiators—in reality, we lose our empathy and compassion. We pay too little attention or none at all to the impact that our actions have on the environment in which we live, on the people around us, and society in general. We dehumanize ourselves.

...

We see the dog-eat-dog attitude every day.

The entrepreneur who ponders how to create a strong need and even how to induce addiction for the product he sells, ignoring the long-term effects on his customers' lives.

The employee who, motivated by the thought of her next promotion, manipulates or undermines her colleagues and bosses.

The manager who, out of a desire to maximize profits and get a bonus, exploits his or her team.

The cab driver who chooses the longer route.

The plumber or the automotive technician who overcharges the customer who doesn't know anything about pipes or cars.

The politician who uses her power or influence for her own gain or the benefit of a small group of individuals.

The lawyer who suggests a particular legal path to follow, the doctor who recommends a specific treatment, the private banker who promotes certain investment products, or the real estate agent who tries to convince his client to buy a certain property—all motivated by the fact that there is a greater financial gain associated with what they propose, without considering whether the proposed solution is the most suitable for the person in front of them.

The Portrait

I've always been fascinated by the central idea of Oscar Wilde's novel *The Picture of Dorian Gray*. The desire of the young and handsome Dorian—for his portrait to age in his place so that he can preserve his beauty—becomes a reality. After his wish is granted, eighteen years pass by in which Dorian surrenders to a hedonistic lifestyle, leading an immoral life and leaving a destructive mark on those around him. The passage of time and his immersion in vice do not produce changes in his appearance, and Dorian remains just as young and handsome. But the portrait becomes unrecognizable: a hideous face as a reflection of a poorly lived life.

...

What if every person had a painting of his or her soul that would allow that individual to see how the core of his or her inner being changes due to daily thoughts, words, and deeds? How it becomes green with envy at the sight of prosperity and good in another person's life and how it burns black with the desire for that person to lose what he or she has. How it inflames like an appendix, until it bursts, when pride and vanity explode in mockery of and contempt for those around. How it writhes and contracts in agonizing spasms under the pressure of greed and selfishness. How it tries to hide its sick color, mimicking an unsuccessful rainbow, pale and weak, when falsehood enters play. How it disintegrates in indifference to the fate of others.

Perhaps such a painting would help us become aware of when our thoughts and actions increase the evil in the world. Intentionally or not.

...

C. S. Lewis: "Pleasure, money, power, and safety are all, as far as they go, good things. The badness consists in pursuing them by the wrong method, or in the wrong way, or too much."[45]

Yes, I plead guilty. I admit that way too many times, I have shown weakness and allowed myself to be dominated by all sorts of negative feelings and moods. I admit that too many times, I have acted foolishly under the tyranny of the endless and insatiable ego.

The Inner Struggle

A vigilante and a predator are hiding in each of us—a hero and a villain. Often, the negative character is stronger. We want to do what we know is right, but we are not strong enough, and our actions are selfish and petty. We aspire to an ideal of justice, kindness, empathy, altruism, and generosity, but we miss every opportunity to approach and grab it. When faced with temptations, self-control melts away, and strength of character dissolves. We sometimes find ourselves in the position of a greedy man who looks with craving eyes at the cookie jar, knowing that he has already eaten his share, reasoning that it will not be the end of the world if he eats just one more cookie . . . and one more, and one more, until he finds himself filled with regret and guilt, staring at the empty jar. How right was the French playwright and historian Jean Racine: "Small crimes always precede the great crime. Whoever has broken the rules once will be capable of trampling on the most sacred of rights. There are different stages in virtue and sin, and innocence has never suddenly collapsed into indecency."[46] In other words, compromise feeds on compromise, and sin feeds on sin. An insignificant wrongdoing committed today paves the way for something more severe tomorrow. And so on, until, at some point, the fall becomes irreversible.

The spiral that takes us away from a well-lived life can be broken by the decision to engage in a continuous struggle with ourselves. With our weaknesses. Choosing to do what is right, no matter how difficult, regardless of costs. A choice that derives from the desire to increase the good and beauty of the world. A choice that arises from the responsibility for everything we received without us having any contribution: the skills, proclivities, and talents with which we were born; the family in which we grew up and the education to which we had access; the unexpected opportunities that suddenly appeared in our lives; the people who extended a helping hand to us when things were bad. This responsibility binds us to act and work for good—not only ours but also the family's and the community's.

...

I don't believe that the inner struggle against flaws and selfish impulses can ever be declared a victory. Rather, it's a war of attrition that I feel obliged to carry on every day and every moment. Hoping that today I will become a slightly better person than I was yesterday, and that progress, no matter how slight, will continue to occur tomorrow.

I am guided by the suggestion of the German philosopher Immanuel Kant: live in such a way that your manner of behaving and acting can become a "universal law," that is, a rule valid for all people.[47] What would happen if this universal law required each of us to give free rein to superficial, primitive, and selfish instincts without discernment? Society would tumble toward self-destruction. Through this perspective, Kant gives us only one viable option, that of always acting right. Aligning our thoughts with our words and our words with our deeds. Removing destructive habits and replacing them with healthier ones. Substituting envy with sincere admiration. Greed with moderation. Selfishness with generosity. Falsehood with authenticity. Indifference with altruism. Vanity with humility. And contempt with respect and acceptance.

Sometimes I fail and suffer a humiliating defeat. Especially at the end of such days, I find very useful an exercise recommended by the practice of Naikan, a method of reflection and self-analysis developed by the Buddhist monk Yoshimoto Ishin.[48] I meditate on three questions: What did I receive today? What did I offer today? What problems or difficulties did I cause today? The goal is not to blame myself and end up drowning in guilt or regret. The goal is to be aware of the impact I have had on those around me. To understand the reasons why I acted the way I did. To identify the weakness that my ego exploited against me. To apologize for the injustice committed and make a firm commitment to repair the damage I've done.

...

I have learned that whatever we put in the world comes back to us like a boomerang, sooner or later, in one form or another. I was often wounded by the very weapons with which my ego had armed me. Torn by greed, bitten by envy, intoxicated by the vapors of pride. Haunted by remorse and regret.

I found that there are times when the price to pay for winning an external battle is far too high. And that on the road to success, sometimes one step back means two steps forward in a much more important journey toward calm and inner peace.

I have discovered that there are moments when the damage done cannot be completely repaired, no matter how hard we try. Like when you hammer a nail into a wall: even if you pull out the nail, the hole remains.

...

"Whatever you want others to be, first be that yourself,"[49] said Paramhansa Yogananda, an Indian spiritual master and yogi. Before we can expect others to treat us with respect, decency, fairness, and friendship, we must be willing to treat those around us the same way, including those who hurt or wronged us.

Pleading for Compassion

Some will not take kindly to everything I have said so far and will argue that I have made a plea for giving up. Stop competing. Stop pursuing external success. Stop acquiring stuff. Or, even worse, stop defending yourself and letting yourself be trampled on when you are mistreated.

Not by a long shot. Instead, it's a plea for kindness or, at the least, for decency. The essence is the following: For a short period, we share this Earth with other people, who, like us, have goals, desires, and dreams that they pursue as best they know and can. If we fail to be of use to them in their journey, the least we can do is not make their journey more difficult.[50]

Moreover, studies indicate that kindness and compassion contribute to success.[51] Regardless of our field, we need others' help to succeed. Managers depend on their teams. Owners of small businesses rely on their employees. Freelancers do not survive without clients. "No man is an island," said the English poet John Donne. The thick-skinned and the scoundrels can achieve their goals by fooling enough people in the short run. However, in the long run, they often end up abandoned and alone.

Last but not least, we should think more often about how we want to remain in the memories of those with whom we cross paths throughout our lives. And behave as such.

...

When we begin to pursue honest living consciously, we learn that sometimes we have to question and even ignore the countless observations, judgments, requests, and desires that assail our minds. When we manage to do this, we find ourselves enveloped by a state of inner stillness. The feeling of calm surrounding you when you watch the lazy dance of the first snowflakes. When the wave of tranquility we bathe in recedes, a new question arises: How can we bring more peace into our hectic lives?

10 | Tranquility

Life as a Script

I was, without realizing it, a director. Imagining, full of hope, how different events should unfold: the next business meeting or important project that could give me my new promotion, the doctor's appointment or the discussion with the real estate agent, the romantic dinner, the weekend in the mountains with my friends, or the vacation with my family. Writing my own script for each episode of life, big or small, all linked together in a linear fashion, without major hurdles and flaws, always with a happy ending. Many times, life had a different perspective, and I found myself suddenly thrown into scenes that I had not anticipated or wanted. Too attached to my imaginary construction of the events, wanting to keep the feeling that I was in control, I reacted instinctively—rejecting the unpredictable, opposing change, desperately clinging to the predetermined scenario. It's no wonder I often wound up frustrated, angry, and anxious.

The Tyrant

All my life, my mind has been inhabited by a little tyrant. Invisible but always present. He is wayward and constantly has something to say. He tells me he likes this and dislikes that. He utters mean and superficial criticisms about everyone, including me. He scolds me, saying that my idea is not good, that others will disapprove of me, or worse, they will laugh at me. Sometimes I feel like he just wants to hurt me, trying to make me feel small and insignificant, comparing me to others, or just telling me I'm not good enough. Quite a few times, he discourages me, saying that it's difficult, that I will not succeed in my attempt, that I'd better give up. Other times, he is downright despicable, rhetorically asking, in a scornful tone, if I really think I deserve more. It's very annoying when he keeps repeating the same thing, like a broken record. Recalling with regret past events that did not have the desired outcome. Visualizing certain life moments that bothered him, analyzing the situation from all perspectives, and criticizing me, saying I should have reacted differently. Or whispering conspiratorially, with an alarmed tone, all sorts of awful things that will surely happen to me in the future. And other times he simply complains about absolutely everything: if it rains, I will ruin my new suit; if it's sunny, it's much too hot; if the manager asks me something during the meeting, the little tyrant inside my head is dissatisfied because the boss is picking on me; if he says nothing, my tyrant feels excluded and ignored.

In time and without realizing it, he became the master of the impulses and habits that push me to act in such a way that I later regret: I stay connected to my social media account long after I've decided to start reading a book; I stop in front of the fast-food joint when I'm on a diet; I buy a gadget on a momentary whim although I promised myself to save more; I get angry when I would like to manage the situation calmly; I am mean, although I would like to have the strength to be kind.

If anyone could hear the constant flow of ideas and thoughts that the little tyrant is tumbling in my mind, he or she would probably say I'm crazy. Or maybe not. After all, we all have that "voice in our head"[52] that gibbers and grumbles all day long. The voice in our heads that we come to identify with ourselves.

The Inner Storm

Behind the mask of calm that we struggle to display in front of others, in each of us, there is an unseen storm triggered by the circumstances in which we find ourselves and the people we interact with. We process over six thousand thoughts a day.[53] We comment, criticize, plan, think about the past, and worry about the future. We face a torrent of moods and emotions—regret, fear, envy, greed, desire, anger. The inner turmoil is exacerbated by everyday noise: we are bombarded from all sides by notifications, information, messages, requests, and emergencies. Sometimes we feel that our mind is like a computer that cannot be disconnected: overloaded and overheated. Other times it seems like a balloon, randomly pushed to and fro by air currents.

In a demanding world where everything moves very fast, we try to find an anchor in ourselves. We fail because of the inner mess reflected outward in the way we act. We let ourselves be guided by emotions, impulses, and instincts. We cling to everything that is pleasing, rejecting anything that causes discomfort. Our answer amplifies the mess, adding a new loop to the spiral that leads to inner chaos.

...

Many people turn to meditation and mindfulness, wanting to be more relaxed, calm, and in control. To gain an advantage that will help them be more efficient, more successful, and ultimately, happier. Studies conducted in recent years show that these are just some of the many benefits of such practices.

The following sections describe basic techniques for focusing the mind and cultivating mindfulness.

Breathe In; Breathe Out

Go to a room where you can be alone. Sit in a comfortable position. Close your eyes and focus on your breathing.[54] Breathe in. Feel the air entering your nose and your abdomen expanding. Breathe out. Feel the air come out and your abdomen compressing. Breathe in. Breathe out.

Soon, your mind will begin to wander without you realizing it, and you will get lost in thoughts and ideas. It's absolutely normal for this to happen. When you notice that your attention is no longer focused on your breathing, break the flow of thoughts and return to the initial activity. Breathe in. Breathe out.

At first, the moments of concentration will be short, a few seconds or dozens of seconds. Don't lose your patience, and don't blame yourself when you observe how easily your mind gets distracted. It's similar to getting upset because a duck quacks or a rabbit has long ears. Every time you find yourself lost in thought, embrace that moment of awareness, and then, slowly, shift your attention to your breathing. With a dose of indulgence and amusement concerning the wandering mind—like a parent witnessing a child's innocent mischief.

Breathe in. Breathe out.

When you find yourself distracted again, you simply come back: breathe in, breathe out. One more time. And again. Patiently. Understanding that this is how you strengthen your attention muscle.

Over time, the moments of concentration will become longer, and a feeling of peace will envelop you. The computer will finally be able to disconnect. In the absence of air currents, the balloon will land smoothly in a sea of tranquility.

Mindfulness

After you learn to keep your attention focused on your breathing, you can move on to the next level.[55]

Start by meditating, as explained previously. When you feel like you have entered a flow that allows you to focus on every inhalation and exhalation, release your attention and allow it to observe whatever is happening outside or inside you.

For example, you hear a noise on the street or in your neighbor's apartment, and at the same time, you are aware that you hear the noise.

You feel an itch on your hand or foot and move your attention to it: you don't scratch; just notice the sensation increasing in intensity, then diminishing and disappearing.

Similarly, you become aware of different sensations in your body: pain in your back or neck, cold feet or warm hands, a particular point of tension. Don't analyze and label them as being good or bad. Simply take note of their presence.

Inevitably, the mind will be invaded by thoughts. Do not try to block them; allow them to unfold and identify them: planning for tomorrow or the weekend, the high value of the loan you have to pay back, the college your child will apply to, the nasty response you got from your boss, which restaurant to order dinner from, how beautiful last year's vacation with the family was. The mind thinks, and you are aware of the existence of every thought that arises. You observe how the mind goes from one idea to another, and you tag along wherever it goes.

Specific thoughts will trigger certain feelings and emotions: fear, unrest, anxiety, anger, lust, joy. Don't reject them or cling to them. Simply turn them into the object of your attention by noting how they manifest in the body: shortness of breath, tightness of heart, an intense sensation of cold or warmth, clenching of teeth or fists, a state of electricity in the stomach area. Don't try to make them disappear. Patiently accept and curiously investigate them. See how the bodily sensations appear and then fade away, taking along the emotions that triggered them.

Sooner or later, you will end up caught in the whirlwind of thoughts, moods, sensations, and emotions. Instead of being aware of their existence, you will be absorbed by them. It's absolutely normal for this to happen. Don't get angry; don't blame yourself; don't be discouraged. All you have to do is start over.

Again focus your attention on breathing so that later, you can allow your mind to roam freely. Go after it, no matter where it takes you.

...

When you practice your hoop throws or soccer kicks, if you try too little or too hard, you end up missing often. In contrast, when you find that optimal zone of effort and concentration, you enter a state of flow that allows you to easily score point after point. With this attitude of relaxed determination, you can make the most of meditation techniques.[56]

...

Over time, you will develop what is known as mindfulness. In other words, the ability to be aware of and recognize everything that is happening around you, but especially inside you. To better understand the difference between being or not being mindful, let's imagine that the inner chaos we often experience—the mixture of impulses, thoughts, moods, and emotions—is like a storm inside a crystal ball. When we are not mindful, we become captive inside the crystal ball: we feel the impact of the unleashed storm and identify with it. When we manage to be aware, we escape from the crystal ball, hold it in our hands, and observe the raging storm within with interest and ease, without identifying with the rain, lightning, thunder, or wind, until they calm down and disappear.

Meditation 2.0

When I first started meditating, I made a mistake that I believe many others also make. Confronted with the unpredictable, the difficulties, and the frustrations that life put in my way, I took shelter in the calm that surrounded me when I sat on the couch, observing my breath. And then, returning to everyday life, I used and exhausted the reserve of tranquility and inner peace to sustain the fight against ambiguity and change, continuing to react impulsively, to cling to what I wanted and reject anything else. I ended up inevitably meditating on the couch, trying to replenish the reserve of calm and inner peace—captive in a never-ending spiral.

I later understood that the primary goal of Buddhist meditation is to help us become accustomed to the concept of impermanence.[57] To accept the transient nature of all that is. After all, when we learn to get out of the crystal ball and watch the storms coming and going, we better understand that nothing lasts. When I assimilated the principle of impermanence, I managed to see the big picture. In a world where change is the only constant, we need to embrace the unknown and ambiguity. To enjoy life without clinging to objects, experiences, or people. To face the difficulties and roadblocks, understanding that if we oppose or reject what is, we only exacerbate the pain and suffering.

Another revelation was this: meditation can bring about radical improvements when we successfully apply its lessons in everyday challenges.[58] The arrogant neighbor, the annoying relative, the two-faced colleague, the abusive boss, the greedy businessman, the power-hungry politician, the situations when we face appealing temptations we want to avoid, the events that cannot be controlled—all these are part of life. Wanting to exclude or make them disappear is unrealistic. It's like dreaming of a constant clear and cloudless sky. Accepting this undeniable truth, when we face the difficulties caused by various external factors, we realize that the best way to respond is to get out of the crystal ball. When we manage to bring the quality of being mindful to everyday events, we learn to detach and look at ourselves as an entirely distinct entity. We visualize the spider's web of thoughts, mental images, desires, and emotions. We observe these without rejecting them, without trying to stop them. We allow them to manifest in the body and watch them form, becoming more and more intense, so that later, their power gradually decreases until they completely fade away. We don't identify with them. We experience the different sensations of anger, unrest, anxiety, craving without becoming angry, fearful, and greedy.[59] We understand the transient nature and lack of substance of all these states, which, left on their own and unassimilated by our ego, lose their grasp on us, becoming a simple smokescreen that appears and vanishes. We realize that between stimulus and response, there is a small blank space that gives us the freedom to choose how we act.[60] This small gap allows us to free ourselves from the tyranny of impulsive reactions and habits—the tyranny of our ego.

The Perfect Effort

Some people misuse the concepts acquired in meditation and develop a state of indifference, lack of concern, or even numbness. They no longer make enough effort to achieve their personal or professional goals, justifying their action— or rather, lack of action—by the desire not to attach and cling to anything, a desire that arose from the misunderstanding of impermanence. Interestingly, before they discovered meditation, these same people were at the opposite pole, fighting with stubbornness and even frustration for every inch that brought them closer to their objective. The same happened in my case. Until the day I understood that the two alternatives are the extreme ends and that the optimal option is somewhere in the middle. And it involves aiming for a single goal: making a perfect effort.[61]

When we commit to making the perfect effort, it does not mean that we have to be perfect, nor that we must achieve the perfect result. It means that in the formula of success and failure, we take into account only one element: if we fought to the last second, if we did everything we could. It doesn't matter if we won or not, if we obtained a lot or very little. Ultimately, the only thing we have complete control over is how we act. All we can do is do all we can. No more, no less. This is where the lessons of Buddhist meditation come into play. We focus on achieving the objective of making the perfect effort without thinking about a specific result that we want. Without anticipating the prizes and applause that might await us at the end. Without clinging to victory and reward.[62] We simply focus on how we act.

This significantly increases our chances of progressing while keeping our inner peace intact.

Inner Peace

The society in which we live and the universe that each of us builds every day for himself or herself take us further and further away from the tranquility we aspire to. Caught in an increasingly fast-paced life, assailed by obligations and demands, motivated by the fear of not missing any opportunity for satisfaction, pleasure, or gain, it becomes harder and harder for us to disconnect.

And yet inner peace is available and can be achieved by anyone willing to try. It all starts with a simple breath. And one more. And one more.

...

Meditation and mindfulness can bring enormous benefits. The storms and commotion of everyday life will never go away. Instead, we become better and more skilled at navigating the storms.

...

Looking at where I started and where I ended up on my journey of self-discovery, I was amazed by the unexpected evolution. The man of the past—smitten, broken, hopeless, and aimless—was gone. He had transformed.

I was ready for the last part of the expedition. Perhaps the most difficult, because I had in front of me a door that had been locked for a long time.

11 | The Closed Door

The Parable of the Sower

"Listen! A farmer went out to sow his seed. As he was scattering the seed, some fell along the path, and the birds came and ate it up. Some fell on rocky places, where it did not have much soil. It sprang up quickly, because the soil was shallow. But when the sun came up, the plants were scorched, and they withered because they had no root. Other seed fell among thorns, which grew up and choked the plants, so that they did not bear grain. Still other seed fell on good soil. It came up, grew and produced a crop, some multiplying thirty, some sixty, some a hundred times. […]

The farmer sows the word. Some people are like seed along the path, where the word is sown. As soon as they hear it, Satan comes and takes away the word that was sown in them. Others, like seed sown on rocky places, hear the word and at once receive it with joy. But since they have no root, they last only a short time. When trouble or persecution comes because of the word, they quickly fall away. Still others, like seed sown among thorns, hear the word; but the worries of this life, the deceitfulness of wealth and the desires for other things come in and choke the word, making it unfruitful. Others, like seed sown on good soil, hear the word, accept it, and produce a crop—some thirty, some sixty, some a hundred times what was sown."[63]

···

The farmer in the parable represents God. The four types of soil represent different human typologies—the various types of soul structures. And the seed is His word. The truth. Which can take strong roots in the human heart and bear fruit. Or go to waste.

···

I easily see myself in the first three situations described in the parable. I was—in different stages of my life—the rocky ground, the thorny ground, or the ground by the road.

In my youth, I blindly took up faith, without sufficiently exploring, without really trying to understand and assimilate what I was taking up. Faced with uncertainties and doubts, instead of looking for answers and clarifications, I preferred to ignore them. Fearful and ashamed that acknowledging the existence of these hesitations would prove how little faith I had. But also because it was easier and more convenient for me to develop a shallow relationship, based on traditions, rituals, and even superstitions, with a God I often regarded like the spirit in Aladdin's lamp. Asking him to help me when I was in need, to fulfill one wish or another.

As I grew older and entered the whirlpool of life, I was assailed by its "worries, by the deceitfulness of wealth, and the desires for other things." Without resisting, I allowed myself to be led, absorbed, and suffocated by everyday anxieties, urges, and pleasures. That didn't leave much time to take care of my soul. To stop the daily commotion and turmoil. Or at least detach myself from it, even for a moment. To humbly admire the flawless beauty of a sunset or the harmonious composition of an autumn storm. To marvel at sometimes lifesaving and unexplainable coincidences. To make a more consistent and profound effort to discover the Artist of the world. To establish a more lasting relationship with Him. My faith, already fragile, built on shaky and unstable ground, gradually eroded.

Confronted with the evil and suffering in the world and my life, I hastily concluded that His work was full of major faults. That the Artist, if He existed, was careless. Or worse, indifferent.

...

Increasingly convinced that there was no one and nothing behind the door, I closed it.[64] I don't remember the exact moment. But I know it's been closed for a long time. Rarely, in critical moments of pain and despair, have I reopened it. I cracked it a little—asking for proof of existence, asking for help. Sometimes begging, other times demanding. Every time, I came across the same answer: dead silence.

The Circle of Life

It is a cold December night, a few days before Christmas. The hospital floor is quiet and gloomy. If not for the voices coming from one of the few patient-occupied rooms, you might think you were in a deserted building.

A woman keeps repeating to the doctor that what he is telling her cannot be true. That she feels the fetus moving. As she's insisting, the doctor double-checks. Trying to calm her down, he tells her the same thing: he is sorry, but the fetus no longer shows any signs of life. The woman doesn't take no for an answer, and she asks to be urgently operated. The doctor agrees and performs a C-section.

As it turned out, the umbilical cord was wrapped around the baby's neck, and he was about to suffocate, barely able to breathe.

I was lucky. I could have been stillborn. Or, due to acute oxygen deprivation, suffered severe physical or mental disabilities. But I was saved.

"This life came so close to never happening."[65]

...

I had been away on business for almost a week. I had kept in touch with my father because my mother's condition had deteriorated in the last few days, and she had been hospitalized. Before I got on the plane, I called him to find out the latest news. He told me that they had moved her to the intensive care unit a few hours ago—to make sure she would get the best support over the weekend. He seemed a bit calmer, which put me at ease a little. My plane landed at night.

The next day we went to the hospital. With our hearts in our mouths. We were barely granted access to the intensive care unit. When we entered the ward where my mother was, I forced myself to smile. For her to see a familiar, friendly, and confident face. We approached; I greeted her and stroked her hair. She stared at us without saying anything. She seemed to be breathing hard. I realized something was wrong. I wanted to fetch a doctor, but at that moment, a cheerful nurse came into the room. Her mood changed as soon as she saw my mother's face, and after looking at the devices and monitors my mother was hooked up to, she told us in a firm and cold voice that we had to leave. Another nurse pointed us to the corridor leading to the exit from the hospital's wing. We stayed there. I could hear the commotion of the nurses and doctors coming in and out of the ward. My father's face, tired, pale, and with dark circles around his eyes, had a strange expression. We were both scared. We saw a nurse passing by in haste and coming back after a few seconds. She was running. She pushed some sort of table with a device on it. I assumed it was a defibrillator. I started praying. It was the only thing left for me to do. I begged God to help us. To forgive me for my vague and meager faith, worn out and tattered, due to my selfishness and doubt. To receive a son's prayer for his mother. To perform a miracle at the last minute. When the hallways were flooded with beeps and other noises coming from devices, I started crying. Thinking about the ordeal my mother had gone through, especially over the last weeks and months, I realized that a more appropriate prayer would have been for what was best for her. She had refused to take the strong painkillers because they were causing her confusion, fogginess, and unconsciousness. I had heard her recently, several times, in fact, saying that she wanted God to take her. When the machines started beeping for the second time, my father came close to me. Trying to prepare me for what he sensed was going to happen, he said to me: "I don't think it's good." He was suffering.

After some time, I don't know how much, a nurse came

and said that the doctor wanted to talk to us. Despite all the evidence, I was still clinging to the hope that things might turn out okay. That my mother could be well and that the disease could go into remission, somehow—I don't know how—in the following period. The doctor was waiting for us in front of the ward. The fifty, sixty feet that separated us seemed infinite to me. The hardest walk I ever had to take. Getting closer, I realized from the expression on the doctor's face that the news was not good. My mother, who was already in a serious condition, had suffered a cardiopulmonary arrest. She was no longer conscious. Her body had given up. The devices were keeping her alive, but not for long. At most, one day. Possibly hours. The doctor told us that we could go in for a few more minutes, if we wanted, and then we had to leave.

I felt exhausted, struck, crushed. I took her hand in mine. It was cold as ice. I said a prayer and bid my farewell. We asked a nurse if we could stay, but she told us no because access to the intensive care unit was restricted and limited.

When I got out, I called my sister. I didn't know if they would let her in. I went to the hospital chapel and found a priest's phone number. I talked to him, and he told me he would send a colleague over as soon as possible.

Thirty minutes later, my sister arrived. Along with my father, she managed to sneak in with one of the people in charge of supplies. In another fifteen minutes, they called to ask me if I could join them. I took advantage when someone from the medical staff opened the door to that wing.

A candle was burning slowly. My mother's hands had been warmed by the grip of her daughter's hands. In the hall of the ward, I heard the voice of a nurse gently telling my father and sister that it might be better for us to leave— to let my mother detach and go on her way. I instinctively looked at the screen, probably showing her heartbeat, and saw the number begin to drop sharply: 62, 53, 43, 31, 20, 9, 0. The nurse approached slowly and told us that she had passed away.

A few moments later, the priest arrived and began to read the prayers for the departed. The three of us, side by side, in front of the bed where my mother was lying.

During her last seconds, she was not alone. I hope she felt our presence.

My mother was born on the thirty-first day of the month. And she died on the thirteenth. A full circle.

Why?

Some people, when seeing the evil and suffering in the world, ask themselves: Why? Why does God allow them to exist and manifest? Isn't God good and loving? Why do we witness—and witness so often—situations in which badness prevails? Isn't God almighty? Why do the innocent fall victim to evil while all sorts of shady and unscrupulous people thrive? Isn't God fair and just?

Confronted with such seemingly unanswerable questions, the faith of many stalls. Because in order to believe, they first need to understand. And the fact that they don't understand is used as an argument to fuel doubts and disbelief.

...

If tomorrow someone brought forth an indisputable proof of God's existence, faith would turn into a simple exercise of logic. Each of us would strive to analyze the newly discovered theorem, and once we understood it, we would cry out with relief: "Aha! It's true. Now I believe!" But what value would such faith have? What value would the deeds of love, generosity, forgiveness, compassion, and help have, no matter how many, if they were done with the thought and certainty that, from somewhere, Someone is watching?

...

Humans, as created beings, cannot have full access to the source and energy from which they were created. To the Artist who designed and built them. To claim to understand the invisible meanings and laws of the world is to claim to transcend one's condition of limited being. Underneath this desire lurks the snake of pride and selfishness. The human who wants to become one with the Artist. The created one wishing to ascend to the same level as the Creator. A reconstruction of the sin that led to Lucifer's fall.[66]

...

Good can only exist in contrast with evil.[67] In a universe in which evil would never have existed and could never exist, the notion of good, as we understand and define it today, would no longer be valid. What significance would the day have in the absence of the night to follow? This means that for good to exist and make sense, the presence of evil is necessary.

...

The world is a battlefield between the two forces of good and evil. Through our everyday words and deeds, we enlist in one of the two sides. Excluding pathological cases— those, few in number, who are unable to differentiate between truth and lie, between justice and injustice—the vast majority of people possess this capacity for understanding. We have and exercise our freedom to choose. Sometimes we choose to act the right way and do good. Other times, we choose evil. And regardless of our reasons or justifications, we do evil knowingly. Because we put ourselves above everyone else. That is, out of selfishness and pride.

···

Some people use the idea of free will to support their arguments against God. Why, they ask, did He create us as beings capable of wickedness, cruelty, and monstrosities?

Let's look at the situation from a different perspective. What would have been the alternative?[68] A human who, faced with temptations, would act the right way. Always. A human built with certain predefined settings. Without actually having the possibility of the wrong choice. In other words, a robot without the freedom to choose, which acts automatically, as guided by its preinstalled software.

Under such conditions, the value of a good deed would be close to nothing. Because the good deed gains power insofar as one actually possesses the freedom to choose the bad deed.

···

God is sometimes judged for the many crimes and atrocities committed by humans against their fellow beings in the name of religion. Our history is full of wars and religious purges. But we lose sight of the fact that God expects faith without asking us to harm and kill in the name of faith. Is it fair to hold Him accountable for the choices and actions of people who have wrongly assimilated the message of love, compassion, forgiveness, and acceptance that underlies the religions of the world?

...

An eye for an eye and a tooth for a tooth. This is the justice that some expect from God. Impatient and unsure of the existence of another world beyond the earthly one, they would like the punishment to be applied here and now. When this is delayed—or worse, when those they see as enemies thrive—they feel disappointed and abandoned. The lack of divine intervention becomes indisputable proof of the nonexistence of God.[69]

We fail to understand that divine reason and logic are different from the human versions.[70] I don't think God uses the prosecutor's accusation techniques or the magistrate's manner of judging. I don't think He only assesses deeds and actions, as we usually do. I believe He also investigates the part that is invisible to us.[71] The essence of a person. His or her soul. The poor woman who gladly and lovingly offers her breakfast to the homeless man can be more generous than the billionaire who donates a million dollars to an NGO for tax-deduction purposes. The man who overcomes his lust and changes his mind at the last moment—overwhelmed with empathy and compassion for the prostitute forced by circumstances to sell her body—is more ethical and kinder than the man who resists the temptation for fear that he might be caught by his wife. The vicious and sadistic CEO who mercilessly exploits his employees, pushing everything to the edge of what is legal, can be more guilty than the leader of a concentration camp, who follows orders mechanically and without thinking for fear of reprisals.

I don't imagine God having a checklist of standard criteria to apply systematically. "His judgment is always circumstantial, adapted to the individual case."[72]

I don't think God is in a hurry; rather, I see Him being tremendously patient with us. Because the most unworthy and the most reprobate person can save his or her soul even in the last seconds of life, in an authentic moment of deeply heartbreaking repentance.[73]

...

Religion teaches that when someone slaps us, we should turn the other cheek.[74] For many, this teaching seems illogical. Does being a believer mean apathetically and inertly accepting injustice? Not responding to abuse and humiliation? No. Religion expects us to put ourselves in the service of good.[75] Condemning unjust deeds and fighting evil without hating the people who commit them.[76] Being aware that justice does not mean revenge. Understanding that if the one who has wronged us is full of regret and sincerely asks us for forgiveness, we owe it to that person with an open heart and without resentment. Realizing that we can forgive only the evil done to us, not having the right to overlook the evil done to our fellow beings.[77] And last but not least, without ever forgetting that human justice and divine justice are two completely different concepts.

...

Mahatma Gandhi was right: "An eye for an eye only ends up making the whole world blind."

Where Is God?

We are so caught up and absorbed in our own existence that we have become shortsighted. We no longer notice the magic and wonder of life unfolding beyond the concrete, buildings, and skyscrapers.

Every time I watch a documentary about life on Earth, I am fascinated by the diversity and complexity I discover. Behind the natural ecosystems, there are complicated but efficient structures that ensure the continuity of life. Every living thing, even the smallest one, represents an amazing composition of systems and processes. Science explains these systems and processes pragmatically using atoms, physical formulas, and chemical reactions. And yet, it's hard to believe that pure chance generated this grand work of art. Serendipity—so that all the necessary conditions to make life on Earth possible were met.

When I ponder that changing any parameter—such as the distance between the sun and the Earth or the atmospheric pressure—would turn Earth into an uninhabitable planet, I realize that I cannot possibly rule out the existence of a higher energy beyond the power of human understanding. A Consciousness that meticulously designed everything, down to the smallest detail. An Artist. God.

...

When we have to choose between acting morally and opting for the less honorable but more beneficial option for us, respectively, we are caught between two impulses. The impulse to do what is right and the impulse to take advantage of the situation. C. S. Lewis observed that, besides the two, there is a third instinct.[78] A sort of internal GPS guiding us. A voice telling us we have the strength to resist temptation. To renounce an easy gain or the satisfaction of a certain pleasure, simply because we know that's the right thing to do. We usually define this instinct using the concept of conscience. Lewis sees here the proof of the divine presence in humans.[79] Indeed, we often ignore the indications of this GPS, allowing urges to take over. After all, the seed sown by the farmer is not quick to take root in our souls, and even then, the root is brittle. But when we do manage to follow the GPS instructions, we increase the good in the world, and with every proof of love, compassion, or forgiveness, we bring to life the divine within us.

...

The following paragraph is part of the story told by former research diver David Bennett, a man who stayed underwater for fifteen to eighteen minutes without breathing and who miraculously survived. The excerpt is reproduced from the documentary *The Story of God with Morgan Freeman*:

"I had totally lost my awareness of my body and the ocean at this point. Then I noticed this light. It was millions upon millions of fragments of light. In all different colors, and they were all dancing and swirling, but kind of like they were one mind, though, and it was infinite. I knew I had left my body, and as I approached this mass of light, it was a familiar home. And it was a relationship that was so much deeper than any relationship I'd ever had here. And then I reached a certain point where these millions of fragments of light spoke. And they said, 'This is not your time. You must return; you have a purpose.' I was watching my body, and I was mesmerized because I knew I was gonna go back in that body."[80]

The vast majority of people who have gone through a near-death experience have similar stories: "a perception of seeing and hearing apart from the physical body, passing into or through a tunnel, encountering a mystical light, intense and generally positive emotions, a review of part or all of their prior life experiences, encountering deceased loved ones, and a choice to return to their earthly life."[81]

Many speak of an overwhelming feeling of unconditional love.[82]

...

A long time ago, I heard a story whose author is anonymous. As the story goes, a very religious woman was praying to God to help her understand what Hell and Heaven look like. One night, an angel appeared in her dream, saying that God had listened to her many prayers. The angel asked if she was prepared to visit Hell. The woman, without hesitation, said yes. Immediately, she saw a room with a large, round table in the middle. On the table, a huge pot full of steaming food. The room was filled with an enticing scent that instantly stimulated your appetite and made you feel hungry. There were several people around the table. Weak, thin, with sunken cheeks, pale, sickly. Sad and desperate. Whining, moaning, screaming. Each held a spoon with a very long handle in his or her hand. So long that they couldn't bring food to their mouths and eat. A few moments later, the angel took the believer to another room to reveal Heaven. Entering with the angel, the woman saw a similar picture: the same large table, the same huge steaming pot, many people around, everyone with spoons with a long handle in their hands. But they looked well fed, healthy, happy, and in a good mood. There was a cheerful atmosphere in the room. The angel, seeing the perplexed believer, explained that the people of Heaven had learned to feed each other with the long spoons. Giving up greed and selfishness.

The Open Door

I was thirteen, maybe fourteen. The boys I played with in my neighborhood, older than me, had learned to swear, throwing around profanities. I didn't want them to think less of me, but I was ashamed to say the vulgar words they shouted at each other in anger. To show them that I was a man, too, I started swearing with a "Go to hell!" or "Damn it!" or "What in the devil's name!" Until I built the bad habit of using these words quite often. From dusk till dawn, I kept saying *hell* or *devil*.

One evening, when I was coming back from school with a group of classmates, one of them suggested we go to church because she had heard from her grandfather that a great bishop was coming on an official visit. When we arrived, the alley in front of the church was flooded with people. We slipped through the crowd. After a while, I noticed, at the end of the alley, a council of priests passing through the flock, holding incense burners in their hands and blessing the congregation. I was overwhelmed with anxiety. Which increased in intensity as the priests approached me. When they got near me, my unrest turned to fear.

I decided to go home and soon recovered. I couldn't explain what had happened. I told myself that I had to stop invoking the devil's name every five words, and for a few weeks, I went to church more often. Then I forgot about this event.

...

A long time ago, my mother gave me a prayer booklet. I put it in the bookcase, and it remained forgotten there. I remembered it shortly after my mother's death. And I've been keeping it at the edge of my bed ever since. Some mornings, after I wake up, I take the prayer booklet and place it on my chest, next to my heart. I just lie there, doing nothing. Sometimes I feel a flow of calm and peace enveloping my body. I can't find any explanation when this happens. And no, I didn't go crazy.

...

We try to understand something that, if it exists, is

beyond our power of understanding. It is true that no one could provide unquestionable evidence to justify the presence of a force beyond human. It is equally true that no one could bring a single piece of evidence that would deny the possibility of God's existence.

For me, this means we can't possibly close the door. And if we can't keep it wide open, for starters, let's keep it a little cracked, at least. Because in order to understand, it may be necessary to believe first. To have a drop of faith. Even as small as a "mustard seed."[83]

12 | Each Passing Moment

Four years ago, I had finished writing the first draft of a book called *30 "Aha" Moments That Will Change Your Life*. A book on how to become more resilient, more efficient, and more productive. On how you can gain an advantage in our ultra-competitive world to achieve the external success you want: money, fame, status. A month later, I reread the manuscript. Something wasn't right, but I couldn't figure out what. I put the sheets of paper in a drawer, and that is where they remained.

Six months ago, when I started working on the book you are reading now, I remembered the thirty "aha" moments. Going through the pages three and a half years after writing them, I found the manuscript quite good, surprisingly. At the same time, I understood what I didn't like about it, which made me give up the project: that was not the book I wanted to write. That was not the message I wanted to put out in the world. Another book on how to reach the peaks of success. I wanted to write about something deeper. But I lacked the necessary life experience—I was unable to articulate the fundamentals.

It took another 110,000,000 seconds to drain from the hourglass of my time. I had to cross through existential storms and deserts. To sink into depression and despair, and find the strength to climb back to the surface. To seek answers to unanswerable questions. At the end of this painful journey, I found the maturity and words that helped me express the message I wanted to put out in the world from the very beginning.

...

Andrei Plesu: "To find what you are looking for, you must first make a long detour, return to yourself from afar, make a journey."[84]

...

When I feel seized and overwhelmed by the world, when I reach a crossroads and I don't know which way to go, or when I become estranged from myself again, I look at the small hourglass on my desk. At the sands of time that drain, slowly but surely, until the upper part is empty. Nothing lasts forever—the impermanence of all that is.

Other times, I imagine what I will reply, at the end of my life, to the questions that should not let us sleep. What did I do with the time I received? How did I take advantage of everything that was offered to me without any personal contribution: skills and talents, chances and opportunities? What did I leave behind me: A drop of good or a puddle of evil? Did I manage to accomplish what life expected of me?

Suddenly, it becomes easier to mute the background noise. To distinguish between accessory and essential. To remember what really matters to me. And to act accordingly.

Sometimes, it takes me awhile to realize I went astray. And that's fine. To return to your path, you must be aware that you are lost. After all, each passing moment is a new opportunity to begin again.[85]

Did You Like *Each Passing Moment*?

Before you go, I want to say thank you for purchasing my book and reading it all the way to the end. Please let me know your opinion of it by providing your review on the Amazon website.

If you believe the book shares an important message, please recommend it to your friends who may be interested in it.

All the best,

Theodor Vik Andreas

About the Author

Theodor Vik Andreas obtained a bachelor's degree in Finance. He started as a stockbroker, then he switched to sales and marketing. His professional career really took off while working as marketing manager and leader for major investing and tech companies in Europe.

He currently follows his passions: writing, investing, entrepreneurship, and volunteering.

Theodor believes in the power of words. His mission as a writer is to improve people's lives and bring a drop of kindness and joy into the world. *Each Passing Moment* is his first book. Theodor's second writing project will be released soon.

References

Albert Camus, The Myth of Sisyphus, trans. Justin O'Brien (Penguin Books, 2013), Kindle.

Andrei Plesu, "Despre problema raului," in Despre inima si alte eseuri (Romania: Humanitas, 2017). (The book is in Romanian; the translation of the title of the essay is "On the Problem of Evil," and the title of the book is On the Heart and Other Essays.)

Andrei Plesu, Parabolele lui Iisus: adevarul ca poveste (Romania: Humanitas, 2017). (The manuscript is in Romanian; the translation of the title is The Parables of Jesus: The Truth as a Story.)

C. S. Lewis, Mere Christianity (HarperOne, 2009), Kindle.

Cameron Crowe, dir., Vanilla Sky (Paramount Pictures, Cruise/Wagner, Vinyl Films, Sogecine, Summit Entertainment, Artisan Entertainment, 2001).

D. Kahneman and A. Deaton, "High Income Improves Evaluation of Life, but Not Emotional Well-Being," Proceedings of the National Academy of Sciences of the United States of America 107, no. 38 (2010): 16489–16493.

Dan Ariely, Predictably Irrational: The Hidden Forces that Shape Our Decisions (HarperCollins, 2009), Kindle.

Dan Harris, 10% Happier: How I Tamed the Voice in My Head, Reduced Stress without Losing My Edge, and Found Self-Help That Actually Works—A True Story (Yellow Kite, 2014), Kindle.

Data from the General Social Survey (GSS), a project of NORC at the University of Chicago.

E. B. Stolzenberg, M. C. Aragon, E. Romo, V. Couch, D. McLennan, M. K. Eagan, and N. Kang, The American Freshman: National Norms Fall, 2019—Expanded Edition (Los Angeles: Higher Education Research Institute, 2020).

Eckhart Tolle, The Power of Now: A Guide to Spiritual Enlightenment (New World Library, 2010), Kindle.

Fernando Savater, Cele zece porunci in secolul al XXI-lea: traditional si actual in mostenirea ramasa de la Moise [The Ten Commandments of the 21st Century, Tradition and Contemporary in the Legacy of Moses], translated from Spanish into Romanian by Coman Lupu (Romania: RAO International Publishing, 2008).

Gabriel Liiceanu, Asteptand o alta omenire (Romania: Humanitas, 2018). (The manuscript is in Romanian; the translation of the title is Waiting for a Different Mankind.)

Gabriel Liiceanu, Usa interzisa (Romania: Humanitas, 2002). (The text is in Romanian, and the translation of the title is The Forbidden Door.)

GBD 2017 Disease and Injury Incidence and Prevalence Collaborators, "Global, Regional, and National Incidence, Prevalence, and Years Lived with Disability for 354 Diseases and Injuries for 195 Countries and Territories, 1990–2017: A Systematic Analysis for the Global Burden of Disease Study," The Lancet 392, no. 10159 (2018): 1789–1858.

Immanuel Kant, Groundwork for the Metaphysics of Morals, trans. Allen W. Wood (Yale University Press, 2002), Kindle.

Individual psychology, attributed to Alfred Adler.

IPBES, Global Assessment Report on Biodiversity and Ecosystem Services of the Intergovernmental Science-Policy Platform on

Biodiversity and Ecosystem Services, ed. E. S. Brondizio, J. Settele, S. Díaz, and H. T. Ngo (Bonn, Germany: IPBES Secretariat, 2019).

J. Tseng, J. Poppenk, Brain meta-state transitions demarcate thoughts across task contexts exposing the mental noise of trait neuroticism, Nat Commun 11, 3480 (2020).

Jean Racine, Phèdre.

Jeffrey Long, "Near-Death Experiences: Evidence for Their Reality," Missouri Medicine 111, no. 5 (2014): 372–380.

Kyriacos C. Markides, The Mountain of Silence: A Search for Orthodox Spirituality (Image, 2002), Kindle.

Mark Epstein, Advice Not Given: A Guide to Getting Over Yourself (Penguin Books, 2018), Kindle.

Mark Epstein, Going to Pieces without Falling Apart: A Buddhist Perspective on Wholeness (Harmony, 2013), Kindle.

Milton Leitenberg, "Deaths in Wars and Conflicts in the 20th Century," Occasional Paper 29, Cornell University, 2006.

Monica C. Worline and Jane E. Dutton, Awakening Compassion at Work: The Quiet Power That Elevates People and Organizations (Berrett-Koehler Publishers, 2017), Kindle.

Nicolae Steinhardt, Jurnalul Fericirii (Romania: Polirom and Rohia Monastery, 2008), ePub format. (The manuscript is in Romanian; the translation of the title is Diary of Happiness.)

Oscar Wilde, The Picture of Dorian Gray.

P. Brickman, D. Coates, and R. Janoff-Bulman, "Lottery Winners and Accident Victims: Is Happiness Relative?" Journal of Personality and Social Psychology 36, no. 8 (1978): 917–927.

Paramhansa Yogananda, How to Be Happy All the Time (Crystal Clarity Publishers, 2006), Kindle.

Pew Research Center

Pleasure principle, attributed to Sigmund Freud.

Raymond Moody, Life After Life: The Bestselling Original Investigation That Revealed "Near-Death Experiences" (HarperOne, 2015), Kindle.

Rick Warren, What on Earth Am I Here For? (from The Purpose Driven Life expanded edition) (Zondervan, 2011), Kindle.

Robert A. Emmons, The Little Book of Gratitude: Create a Life of Happiness and Wellbeing by Giving Thanks (Gaia, 2016), Kindle.

Spike Lee, dir., 25th Hour (25th Hour Productions, 40 Acres and A Mule Filmworks, Gamut Films, Industry Entertainment, Touchstone Pictures, 2002).

Stories from the website of the Near-Death Experience Research Foundation (NDERF), founded by Jeffrey Long, medical doctor, and Jody Long, attorney.

T. W. Crowther, H. B. Glick, K. R. Covey, C. Bettigole, D. S. Maynard, S. M. Thomas, J. R. Smith, G. Hintler, M. C. Duguid, G. Amatulli, M.-N. Tuanmu, W. Jetz, C. Salas, C. Stam, D. Piotto, R. Tavani, S. Green, G. Bruce, S. J. Williams, S. K. Wiser, M. O. Huber, G. M. Hengeveld, G.-J. Nabuurs, E. Tikhonova, P. Borchardt, C.-F. Li, L. W. Powrie, M. Fischer, A. Hemp, J. Homeier, P. Cho, A. C. Vibrans, P. M. Umunay, S. L. Piao, C. W. Rowe, M. S. Ashton, P. R. Crane, and M. A. Bradford, "Mapping Tree Density at a Global Scale," Nature 525, (2015): 201–205.

Tal Ben-Shahar, Happier: Learn the Secrets to Daily Joy and Lasting

Fulfillment (McGraw-Hill Education, 2007), Kindle.

The NIV Bible Translation, Biblica, the International Bible Society.

The Story of God with Morgan Freeman, season 1, episode 1, "Beyond Death" (Revelations Entertainment, 2016).

The World Bank.

Thomas Carter, dir., When the Game Stands Tall (Affirm Films, Mandalay Pictures, 2014).

Viktor E. Frankl, Man's Search for Meaning (Beacon Press, 2006), Kindle.

World Health Organization.

World Wildlife Fund, Living Planet Report, ed. R. E. A. Almond, M. Grooten, and T. Petersen (Gland, Switzerland: World Wildlife Fund, 2020).

Notes

[1] See Gabriel Liiceanu, *Usa interzisa* (Romania: Humanitas, 2002), 176–181. (The text is in Romanian, and the translation of the title is *The Forbidden Door*.)

[2] See Albert Camus, *The Myth of Sisyphus*, trans. Justin O'Brien (Penguin Books, 2013), 11–13, Kindle.

[3] The exercise was recommended by one of my acquaintances. Unfortunately, I was unable to find the original source to give an attribution. Contemplating one's mortality was recommended by the ancient Stoic philosophers. Today, several religions, including Buddhism, encourage people to think about and contemplate death and mortality.

[4] For more on dealing with difficult emotions, please see Mark Epstein, *Advice Not Given: A Guide to Getting Over Yourself* (Penguin Books, 2018), 68–82, Kindle.

[5] This is the applied exercise called RAIN (**R**ecognize, **A**llow, **I**nvestigate, **N**onidentification). For details, please see Dan Harris, *10% Happier: How I Tamed the Voice in My Head, Reduced Stress without Losing My Edge, and Found Self-Help That Actually Works—A True Story* (Yellow Kite, 2014), 112–113, Kindle.

[6] Impermanence is a key element of Buddhist philosophy.

[7] See Gabriel Liiceanu, *Asteptand o alta omenire* (Romania: Humanitas, 2018), 15. (The manuscript is in Romanian; the translation of the title is *Waiting for a Different Mankind*.) Liiceanu uses the expression "fear, hunger, and sex" when he is talking about the elements that lead to less moral actions.

[8] Evolutionary psychologists consider that human behavior is driven by the physical and psychological aspects of evolution meant to help our ancestors survive and reproduce.

[9] E. B. Stolzenberg, M. C. Aragon, E. Romo, V. Couch, D. McLennan, M. K. Eagan, and N. Kang, *The American Freshman: National Norms Fall, 2019—Expanded Edition* (Los Angeles: Higher Education Research Institute, 2020).

[10] Pew Research Center, "A Portrait of 'Generation Next': How Young People View Their Lives, Futures and Politics," January

2007,   https://www.pewresearch.org/politics/2007/01/09/a-portrait-of-generation-next/.

[11] See Tal Ben-Shahar, *Happier: Learn the Secrets to Daily Joy and Lasting Fulfillment* (McGraw-Hill Education, 2007), 16–20, Kindle.

[12] See Tal Ben-Shahar, *Happier,* 20–23.

[13] See Tal Ben-Shahar, *Happier*, 26.

[14] GBD 2017 Disease and Injury Incidence and Prevalence Collaborators, "Global, Regional, and National Incidence, Prevalence, and Years Lived with Disability for 354 Diseases and Injuries for 195 Countries and Territories, 1990–2017: A Systematic Analysis for the Global Burden of Disease Study," *The Lancet* 392, no. 10159 (2018): 1789–1858.

[15] Pew Research Center analysis of data from the 2017 National Survey on Drug Use and Health.

[16] Data from the General Social Survey (GSS), a project of NORC at the University of Chicago.

[17] Analysis of data from the World Bank.

[18] D. Kahneman and A. Deaton, "High Income Improves Evaluation of Life, but Not Emotional Well-Being," *Proceedings of the National Academy of Sciences of the United States of America* 107, no. 38 (2010): 16489–16493.

[19] P. Brickman, D. Coates, and R. Janoff-Bulman, "Lottery Winners and Accident Victims: Is Happiness Relative?" *Journal of Personality and Social Psychology* 36, no. 8 (1978): 917–927.

[20] See Andrei Plesu, *Parabolele lui Iisus: adevarul ca poveste* (Romania: Humanitas, 2017), 11–13. (The manuscript is in Romanian; the translation of the title is *The Parables of Jesus: The Truth as a Story*.)

[21] I first saw this visual example of relativity here Dan Ariely, *Predictably Irrational: The Hidden Forces that Shape Our Decisions* (HarperCollins, 2009), 22, Kindle.

[22] The World Bank.

[23] See Robert A. Emmons, *The Little Book of Gratitude: Create a Life of Happiness and Wellbeing by Giving Thanks* (Gaia, 2016), 19–21, Kindle.

[24] World Health Organization.

[25] World Health Organization.

[26] World Health Organization.

[27] See Rick Warren, *What on Earth Am I Here For? (from The Purpose Driven Life expanded edition)* (Zondervan, 2011), 12–

15, 42–44, 51–55, Kindle.

[28] See Andrei Plesu, "Despre problema raului," in *Despre inima si alte eseuri* (Romania: Humanitas, 2017), 124–126. (The book is in Romanian; the translation of the title of the essay is "On the Problem of Evil," and the title of the book is *On the Heart and Other Essays.*)

[29] Job 1:21, the NIV Bible Translation, Biblica, the International Bible Society.

[30] Pew Research Center analysis of survey data from the United States and more than two dozen other countries.

[31] See Albert Camus, *The Myth of Sisyphus,* 38–41.

[32] The concept of the pleasure principle, attributed to Sigmund Freud.

[33] As postulated by individual psychology and attributed to Alfred Adler.

[34] See Viktor E. Frankl, *Man's Search for Meaning* (Beacon Press, 2006), 76–77, Kindle.

[35] See William J. Winslade, "Afterword," in Viktor E. Frankl, *Man's Search for Meaning*, 164–165.

[36] See Viktor E. Frankl, *Man's Search for Meaning*, 64–66, 147–148.

[37] See "Preface to the 1992 Edition," in Viktor E. Frankl, *Man's Search for Meaning.*

[38] See Tal Ben-Shahar, *Happier*, 129–134.

[39] See Viktor E. Frankl, *Man's Search for Meaning*, 120–121, 150.

[40] T. W. Crowther, H. B. Glick, K. R. Covey, C. Bettigole, D. S. Maynard, S. M. Thomas, J. R. Smith, G. Hintler, M. C. Duguid, G. Amatulli, M.-N. Tuanmu, W. Jetz, C. Salas, C. Stam, D. Piotto, R. Tavani, S. Green, G. Bruce, S. J. Williams, S. K. Wiser, M. O. Huber, G. M. Hengeveld, G.-J. Nabuurs, E. Tikhonova, P. Borchardt, C.-F. Li, L. W. Powrie, M. Fischer, A. Hemp, J. Homeier, P. Cho, A. C. Vibrans, P. M. Umunay, S. L. Piao, C. W. Rowe, M. S. Ashton, P. R. Crane, and M. A. Bradford, "Mapping Tree Density at a Global Scale," *Nature* 525, (2015): 201–205.

[41] IPBES, *Global Assessment Report on Biodiversity and Ecosystem Services of the Intergovernmental Science-Policy Platform on Biodiversity and Ecosystem Services*, ed. E. S. Brondizio, J. Settele, S. Díaz, and H. T. Ngo (Bonn, Germany: IPBES Secretariat, 2019).

[42] World Wildlife Fund, *Living Planet Report*, ed. R. E. A.

Almond, M. Grooten, and T. Petersen (Gland, Switzerland: World Wildlife Fund, 2020).

[43] See Fernando Savater, *Cele zece porunci in secolul al XXI-lea: traditional si actual in mostenirea ramasa de la Moise* [*The Ten Commandments of the 21st Century, Tradition and Contemporary in the Legacy of Moses*], translated from Spanish into Romanian by Coman Lupu (Romania: RAO International Publishing, 2008), 30.

[44] Milton Leitenberg, "Deaths in Wars and Conflicts in the 20th Century," Occasional Paper 29, Cornell University, 2006.

[45] See C. S. Lewis, *Mere Christianity* (HarperOne, 2009), 43–44, Kindle.

[46] This is the translation of the French text "Quelques crimes toujours précèdent les grands crimes. Quiconque a pu franchir les bornes légitimes peut violer enfin les droits les plus sacrés. Ainsi que la vertu, le crime a ses degrés, et jamais on n'a vu la timide innocence passer subitement à l'extrême licence," from *Phèdre*, a classical tragedy in five acts, written by Jean Racine in 1677.

[47] See Gabriel Liiceanu, *Asteptand o alta omenire*, 31–32. Also, Kant notes, "I ought never to conduct myself except so that I could also will that my maxim become a universal law"; see Immanuel Kant, *Groundwork for the Metaphysics of Morals*, trans. Allen W. Wood (Yale University Press, 2002), Kindle.

[48] I first found information about Naikan practice in Robert A. Emmons, *The Little Book of Gratitude*, 39–40.

[49] See Paramhansa Yogananda, *How to Be Happy All the Time* (Crystal Clarity Publishers, 2006), chapter 4, Kindle.

[50] Dalai Lama XIV: "If you can, help others; if you cannot do that, at least do not harm them."

[51] See Monica C. Worline and Jane E. Dutton, *Awakening Compassion at Work: The Quiet Power That Elevates People and Organizations* (Berrett-Koehler Publishers, 2017), Kindle.

[52] See Eckhart Tolle, *The Power of Now: A Guide to Spiritual Enlightenment* (New World Library, 2010), 17–18, Kindle. Also, according to Mark Epstein, the third step of the Buddhist Eightfold Path—right speech—refers not only to how we talk to others but also to how we talk to ourselves. In this view, right speech asks us to question the "repetitive and destructive patterns of thinking that drag us into circular eddies of criticism and blame, often with our self, or those close to us, as the target." See Mark Epstein,

Advice Not Given, 65–66.

[53] J. Tseng, J. Poppenk, *Brain meta-state transitions demarcate thoughts across task contexts exposing the mental noise of trait neuroticism*, Nat Commun 11, 3480 (2020).

[54] See Mark Epstein, *Advice Not Given*, 20, 169–170.

[55] See Mark Epstein, *Advice Not Given,* 20, 149–150.

[56] See Mark Epstein, *Advice Not Given,* 123–124.

[57] See Mark Epstein, *Advice Not Given,* 19–27.

[58] See Mark Epstein, *Advice Not Given*, 13–14. See also Mark Epstein, *Going to Pieces without Falling Apart: A Buddhist Perspective on Wholeness* (Harmony, 2013), 127–131, Kindle.

[59] This is the applied exercise called RAIN mentioned in note 5; for details, please see Dan Harris, *10% Happier*, 112–113.

[60] See Dan Harris, *10% Happier*, 115.

[61] The concept of "perfect effort" was at the core of Bob Ladouceur's coaching philosophy. Under his command, the De La Salle High School Spartans obtained a 151-game winning streak, an incredible performance not only in the world of American football but also in the world of sports in general. See Thomas Carter, dir., *When the Game Stands Tall* (Affirm Films, Mandalay Pictures, 2014).

[62] See Dan Harris, *10% Happier*, 205–207.

[63] Mark 4:3–20, the NIV Bible Translation, Biblica, the International Bible Society.

[64] I first found the concept of "opened/closed doors," from a spiritual and religious perspective, in Andrei Plesu, *Parabolele lui Iisus*, 245–258.

[65] Line from the end of the movie *25th Hour*. Spike Lee, dir., *25th Hour* (25th Hour Productions, 40 Acres and A Mule Filmworks, Gamut Films, Industry Entertainment, Touchstone Pictures, 2002).

[66] Isaiah 14:12–15.

[67] See Andrei Plesu, "Despre problema raului," in *Despre inima si alte eseuri*, 131–132.

[68] See C. S. Lewis, *Mere Christianity*, 47–48.

[69] See Kyriacos C. Markides, *The Mountain of Silence: A Search for Orthodox Spirituality* (Image, 2002), 175, Kindle.

[70] See Kyriacos C. Markides, *The Mountain of Silence*, 175–176. See also Andrei Plesu, *Parabolele lui Iisus*, 212.

[71] See C. S. Lewis, *Mere Christianity*, 79–80, 90–93.

[72] See Andrei Plesu, *Parabolele lui Iisus*, 212.

[73] See Andrei Plesu, "Despre problema raului," in *Despre inima si alte eseuri*, 144–148. See also Andrei Plesu, *Parabolele lui Iisus*, 240–241.

[74] Matthew 5:38–41.

[75] See Kyriacos C. Markides, *The Mountain of Silence*, 176–177.

[76] See C. S. Lewis, *Mere Christianity*, 115–120.

[77] See Nicolae Steinhardt, *Jurnalul Fericirii* (Romania: Polirom and Rohia Monastery, 2008), 119–120, ePub format. (The manuscript is in Romanian; the translation of the title is *Diary of Happiness*.)

[78] See C. S. Lewis, *Mere Christianity*, 9–15.

[79] See C. S. Lewis, *Mere Christianity*, 21–25.

[80] Fragment extracted from *The Story of God with Morgan Freeman*, season 1, episode 1, "Beyond Death" (Revelations Entertainment, 2016).

[81] Jeffrey Long, "Near-Death Experiences: Evidence for Their Reality," *Missouri Medicine* 111, no. 5 (2014): 372–380. See also Raymond Moody, *Life After Life: The Bestselling Original Investigation That Revealed "Near-Death Experiences"* (HarperOne, 2015), Kindle.

[82] Stories from the website of the Near-Death Experience Research Foundation (NDERF), founded by Jeffrey Long, medical doctor, and Jody Long, attorney.

[83] Matthew 17:14–23, the NIV Bible Translation, Biblica, the International Bible Society.

[84] See Andrei Plesu, *Parabolele lui Iisus*, 15.

[85] I was inspired by the line "Every passing minute is another chance to turn it all around" from the movie *Vanilla Sky*. Cameron Crowe, dir., *Vanilla Sky* (Paramount Pictures, Cruise/Wagner, Vinyl Films, Sogecine, Summit Entertainment, Artisan Entertainment, 2001).

Printed in Great Britain
by Amazon